# JOURNEY BACK TO EDEN

# JOURNEY BACK TO EDEN

## My Life and Times among the Desert Fathers

MARK GRUBER, O.S.B.

Transcribed and edited by
M. Michele Ransil, C.D.P.

SVA

2002

fr Mark Gruber. OSB

ORBIS BOOKS

Maryknoll, New York 10545

Uncredited photographs are by Father Mark Gruber, O.S.B. Thanks to Father John Watson for use of several of his photographs.

Frontispiece: The cave entrance of a hermit monk; note the skylight opened above.

Founded in 1970, Orbis Books endeavors to publish works that enlighten the mind, nourish the spirit, and challenge the conscience. The publishing arm of the Maryknoll Fathers & Brothers, Orbis seeks to explore the global dimensions of the Christian faith and mission, to invite dialogue with diverse cultures and religious traditions, and to serve the cause of reconciliation and peace. The books published reflect the views of their authors and do not represent the official position of the Maryknoll Society. To learn more about Maryknoll and Orbis Books, please visit our website at www.maryknoll.org.

---

Published by Orbis Books, Maryknoll, NY 10545-0308.

Imprimi Potest: Rt. Rev. Douglas R. Nowicki, Archabbot, Saint Vincent Archabbey, Latrobe, Pennsylvania

Manufactured in the United States of America

---

**Library of Congress Cataloging-in-Publication Data**

Gruber, Mark, O.S.B.
  Journey back to Eden : my life and times among the desert fathers /
Mark Gruber ; transcribed and edited by M. Michele Ransil.
       p. cm.
  ISBN 1-57075-433-0 (pbk.)
  1. Monasticism and religious orders, Coptic—Egypt. 2. Gruber, Mark,
O.S.B.—Journeys—Egypt. 3. Gruber, Mark, O.S.B.—Diaries. 4.
Egypt—Description and travel. I. Ransil, M. Michele. II. Title.
  BX137.2 .G78 2002
  271'.8172—dc21

2002004227

In gratitude to Abuna Elia,
the saintly desert monk who called me his "Isaac,"
and commissioned me to make his life fruitful
by absorbing the words he had treasured in his heart
in his years of solitude,
and bringing them to fruition
in my own heart and monastic ministry.

*In this deadly 130-degree heat wave,*
*the old monk was actually singing!*
*He was singing a song filled with praise and thanksgiving*
*for the wonder and the beauty*
*of the day I was accursing!*
*He was able to see an Eden*
*in the midst of this wretched desert!*

*—"A Time for Farewells"*

# CONTENTS

# PREFACE

While in Egypt, I did not intend to keep a spiritual journal. My immediate, practical goal was to spend a year doing ethnographic fieldwork in order to write a dissertation for a doctorate in anthropology. My abbot had commissioned me to this end so that I could teach at the college affiliated with my Benedictine monastery. My academic mission and scholastic zeal precluded the writing of elaborate spiritual reflections in those days.

But in spite of myself, the intensity of the faith of those among whom I lived and traveled compelled me to scribble little notes in the margins, or as parentheses in my ethnographic notes, or to make unexpected excursions into religious meditations while otherwise doing my "social science."

Some years ago, my colleague in pastoral publication, Sister Michele Ransil, C.D.P., urged me to distill a desert journal from my notebooks for the readers of our earlier books. Half-heartedly I agreed, but once I began editing my notes, I had to relive experiences that were still painful, as I had never really come to terms with the loss of those days. So, I gave up on the enterprise. However, as time went on, people who regularly attend the retreats I offer began to pressure me to once again take up the task of journal-making.

Here, then, after two years of sporadic labor, is the result. Compiled together, this gives the appearance of being a coherent text. But that is not the case. No such journal as this existed on my person, or in my possessions, when I returned from Egypt. It has been gleaned from haphazardly written comments, letters retrieved from my family, stories of my desert sojourn recorded during retreats, footnotes from early drafts of my dissertation, and archived interviews. Some of my notebooks contain efforts at recording impressions in Arabic. Using a tape recorder, I translated these notes into English. The notes were transcribed and, along with all my other scribblings, input into a computer.

With these raw materials, I reconstructed a time line and, from memory, supplied the connecting tissue of the content. This work is as much a product of the journal-keeping genre as the fact thereof. I offer it because the medium of friendship is the proper ambiance in which to preach, teach, or witness the Gospel. But friendship is a medium of self-disclosure and interest in the other. The friends who have heard me preach or teach, and believe my witness of faith rightly wish to know about this formative and mysterious part of my life, otherwise so inaccessible to them.

I hasten, then, to insist that this is a journal effort that reveals far more of me than of the cultural context or religious setting in which I sojourned. Coptic readers may no doubt assert that I have taken elements of their world and repackaged them in terms of mine. Guilty! I can only reply that a journal, by its very nature, does not have to be an ethnography.

Nevertheless, I hasten to assure all readers—Copts, retreatants, or others—that my respect for the monks among whom I lived and the Coptic people I studied is boundless. I apologize if any remark or perspective seems less reverent than what I intended. I am fully aware that cultural differences between Coptic Egypt and the post-Christian West are so great that even the most respectful treatment of the religion of one by the other will always be problematic. In addition, the years have dulled the powers of my memory so that errant information may have entered the record; linguistic limitations and cultural prejudices may even have confused my initial personal impressions. While I have tried to minimize such occurrences, this, too, is the stuff of journals!

No Coptic prelate has authorized this journal as a reliable guide to his religion, and no pretense is here made that this effort attempts to expedite the ecumenical process of Catholic-Coptic reconciliation. Nevertheless, my gratitude to Coptic abbots, bishops, monks, and their laity is beyond measure.

I am especially grateful to His Holiness, Pope Shenouda III, whose hospitality opened the doors of the desert monasteries to my visitation and who took time to visit me there with words of wisdom and kindness. I likewise thank Sister Michele, who gently shepherded me through this process of compilation and revision. And I could not complete a preface justly without thanking Abuna

Elia, to whom this journal is dedicated, a true mentor of faith for me. I also thank the Kamal-Hanna family of Heliopolis who graciously hosted me so often in Cairo, just as St. Bishoi Monastery under Bishop Serabamon hosted me during my longest stay in the desert. Others also, too numerous to mention, have my life-long gratitude for the role they played during that fateful year in Egypt.

On the local scene, I am indebted to my confrere, Fr. Mark Wenzinger, O.S.B., for his insightful comments on the text, and most especially to Kerry Crawford, who willingly assumed the time-consuming task of proofreading the manuscript.

Finally, a word about the problem of scriptural citations. The biblical verses quoted in this journal are often the stuff of memory reconstruction, involving the subjective process of juggling multiple translations from several languages. No attempt has been made to "homogenize" the varied biblical passages quoted herein and, therefore, no crediting of sources is possible.

> Feast of the Assumption of the Virgin Mary
> August 15, 2001

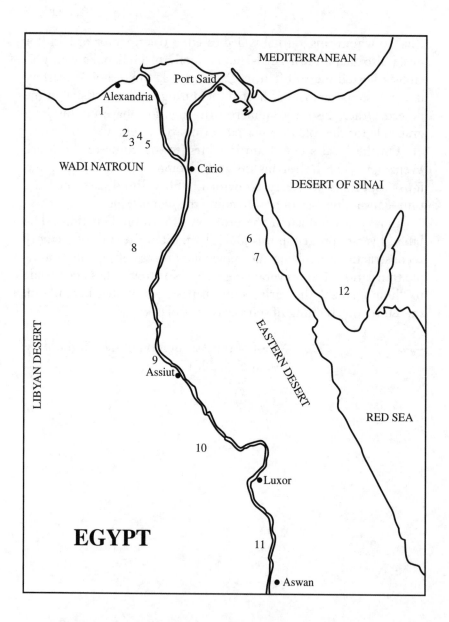

MEDITERRANEAN

Port Said

Alexandria
1

2 4
3 5

WADI NATROUN

● Cario

DESERT OF SINAI

8

6

7

12

LIBYAN DESERT

EASTERN DESERT

9
Assiut●

RED SEA

10

●Luxor

EGYPT

11

● Aswan

## COPTIC MONASTERIES VISITED BY THE AUTHOR

1. Monastery of St. Mari Mina
2. Monastery of el Baramous
3. Monastery of el Suriani
4. Monastery of St. Bishoi
5. Monastery of St. Macarius
6. Monastery of St. Anthony
7. Monastery of St. Paul
8. Monastery of St. Samuel
9. Monastery of el Muharraq
10. Monastery of St. George
11. Monastery of St. Pachomius
12. Monastery of St. Catherine

# ABOUT THE COPTS AND THEIR DESERT MONASTERIES

Egypt is not a homogenous Arab and Islamic nation. A sizable minority of an indigenous stock (the term "Copt" is a cognate of E-"gypt") has maintained a Christian faith since the Apostolic era. The Copts followed an early medieval pattern of the late imperial Roman provinces which sought autonomy from Byzantine control and formed ethnic, ecclesiastical enclaves, often ostensibly over theological disputes. But before the Coptic Orthodox Church differentiated itself from its larger Mediterranean religious context, it provided to Christianity the witness of a dramatic and profound movement of the Spirit: monasticism.

Monasticism, as an eremitical (solitary life) or a cenobitical (communal life) ideal, arose first in Egypt well before the reign of Constantine in the West, and two centuries before St. Benedict codified it in his *Rule*. The "Desert Fathers," as well as "Mothers," have inspired generations of Christians from the fourth century down to our own. And while the Latin Church and the Eastern Orthodox Churches progressively lost track of Egypt after schisms and Islamic occupation, the Coptic faith continued, and monasticism flourished there through the ages until the present.

Modern Copts no longer speak the ancient Pharaonic tongue, but they use it liberally in their liturgical rites. As a whole, the Copts are relatively devout in the exercise of their Faith, and cautious about their minority status in their assertively Islamic world. Economically, they hold paradoxical roles on the margins of a society wherein advantages and disadvantages are both evident. But the desert monastery is the spiritual homeland of the Copts. They honor its heroic inhabitants; they count on their prayers; and they visit it in pilgrimage.

*The author with Mount Horeb in the background.*

# INTRODUCTION

## Bon Voyage!

AUGUST 30, SATURDAY

One more day and the long-awaited adventure begins—the realization of all my plans, fascination, and foreboding: Egypt. In spite of all my research, Egypt is more mythology to me than geography. It is a land of compounded mysteries, layered like the mud of the endless cycle of Nilotic floods: the Pharaonic Egypt of monumental tombs and temples; the Ptolemaic Egypt of Alexandria's library and its lighthouse; the Roman Egypt of Cleopatra and the imperial granary; the Coptic Egypt of desert monks and heroic martyrdoms; the Byzantine Egypt of imperial excess and decay; the Arabic Egypt of Islamic mosques and minarets; the Turkish Egypt of Mamelukes and black coffee; the British Egypt of prime ministers and the Suez Canal; and the national Egypt of the Aswan High Dam and ethnic, Arab restoration: the flip side of the Israeli miracle of ancient peoples, now re-emergent.

While in my mind the history is neatly stratified like the Nile's alluvial deposits, for the Egyptian it must be more organic, each living layer interpenetrating and informing the other. Such a people must carry a heavy weight of memory, not necessarily from an explicit awareness of their history, but from the gravity of history itself.

An immense weight of resignation, if not fatalism, presses on the shoulders of ancient peoples. In terms of politics, Americans are citizens of a fairly old government, but culturally we are a relatively new people. We think in terms of social experimentation, future visions, and great new horizons. Old peoples are profoundly humble about the future, modest about change, and perhaps more forgiving of the weaknesses of the past.

1

I will be traveling into the midst of an old people, where my orientation as an American will serve me far less than the deeper orientation I have as a Catholic. It is an orientation that is rare in my generation, and even in many of the institutions of my Church. I have learned to become forgiving of the sins of the past, unlike the Protestant heart of my nation and its national Churches. I do not wish to repudiate everybody and every thing. History must be more than an exposé, more than a radical critique and dismissal. Surely history—Catholic history, at least, like the living history of Egypt—must seek to reclaim the good and the true of the past. Certainly biblical history does. Which generation of Israel excommunicated the former generation for all its sins, and sought to reinvent the Covenant? Which heir of King David repudiated his ancestor and sought to set up another line? Even Jesus came to fulfill, not to abolish.

So I go to Egypt, knowing that everything I discover is a rediscovery of something timeless and old. Old things and ancient themes quicken in me as I get ready to go. St. Mark, my patron saint, was Egypt's first evangelist and apostolic patriarch. St. Benedict, the founder of my monastic order, derived his idea of monastic life from Egypt's Desert Fathers. Benedictine monasticism is desert-rooted till now. Even the name of Infant Jesus Church, where I have been living and working in residence for the past three years, reminds me of our Savior's childhood in Egyptian exile. *Out of Egypt I have called my son* (Hosea 11:1).

Suddenly I feel that I have been hemmed in, that the selection of my area of anthropological research was no accident at all. Something in the solitariness of my temperament and the abstracted look of my face has the feel of finally making the pilgrimage all men must make. I am becoming the refugee we all must become in order to come home.

### An Accident or Providence?

How has it happened that my doctoral research is sending me off to Egypt? What were the "accidental" details that have conspired to send me into exile in the desert for a whole year?

I well remember the scenario, how the monks of St. Vincent Archabbey pressed me to hurry the pace of my studies. My graduate classmates have been in doctoral programs for nearly a decade, but by the end of just one year, my confreres were asking when I would be finishing my dissertation! So I hastened my program as much as I could, thereby taking courses out of their proper sequence.

So it happened that in my second year, I appeared in a dissertation methodology class, quite ahead of schedule, in an attempt to finish my course work early. Madame Professor walked in, eyed us all dubiously, and announced: "This class is only for advanced graduate students preparing their dissertations or proposals for fieldwork" (read "ethnographic fieldwork," that year-long, intensive, participant-observation, cultural research for which anthropology is famous). She went on to say: "If you do not have a dissertation topic, and if you have not already compiled a bibliography and completed a considerable amount of research, please leave the class now!"

I sat there motionlessly, suspended between two conflicting poles of authority. Before my face, my professor said "Leave!" In my mind, my abbot said, "Hurry up your course work; stay!" I hesitated long enough for the professor to assume my compliance with her command. She looked about and said, "Fine. We're all still here." Then, looking straight at me, she said, *"You,* for instance, what is *your* topic?"

Without thinking, I blurted out, "Egypt. I shall investigate the Coptic people of Egypt."

"Oh!" she exclaimed in utter disbelief. *"Really!* Tell me about them."

In fact, I knew almost nothing of what I spoke! I had considered no dissertation topic and had done no research. But as "fate" would have it, that very morning, as I surveyed the pastor's antique collection of *National Geographic* magazines while sipping a cup of coffee, I happened to pick up an issue featuring the wonders of the Nile. Somewhere deep in the text, I noted a small picture of a Christian Copt. A little blurb stated that these people number about ten percent of the population in Egypt; that there are still monasteries there dating back to the beginnings of monasticism; and that the Copts still practice their ancient form of Orthodox religion. I read the article with little interest, put the journal back in its place, and went to class.

This is what popped into my head when the professor asked for my dissertation topic. I had read the works of the Desert Fathers in my novitiate and had some vague recollection of the maxims of the early monks. I mentally tied all that together with the Copts of Egypt, hoping that they were the same people. So, armed with these two bits of insight, a bit of general knowledge, and a large dose of speculation, I answered my professor's litany of questions for more than fifteen minutes and finally persuaded her that, indeed, I did belong in the class!

By the end of the semester, the work which I was required to do to stay in the class had accumulated sufficiently to enable me to keep the topic I had invented on the spot. This was seemingly an accident and yet, by now, it feels as if it was inevitable.

Which of Joseph's many brothers was held captive in Egypt as a ruse to bring his father, Jacob, out of Palestine for a reunion? I am like that brother, now held captive by a ruse of my own. Or could it be that God, who is the cleverest of all, has played tricks on my tricks to accomplish his will?

# SEPTEMBER
## A TIME OF UNCERTAINTY

### *First Impressions*

SEPTEMBER 3, WEDNESDAY

My plane landed two days ago in Alexandria. It's unusual to fly to Egypt and land in Alexandria rather than in Cairo, I gather, though it seemed to me to be a good idea to come first to the city which is more ancient; to enter Egypt through its historical door, and then to go later to Cairo. Besides, Father Douglas, one of the monks at St. Vincent's, has some contacts in Alexandria and he thought it would be good for me to come to Egypt by being welcomed in Alexandria first.

My host for the moment, a doctor, is ambivalent toward me. He is very gracious, even excessively so on some external level, but when I speak about the work I'm doing, he seems uncomfortable. He says things like, "The Copts are the past of Egypt. A venerable institution," he calls them, "which everyone reverences, but it is not the living Egypt. The living Egypt is Islamic and Arabic." He doesn't understand who I am at all. When the time comes in a meal to offer toasts or extend good wishes, he even keeps proposing that I might one day find a fine wife and have many kids, although I'm sure he knows I'm a priest.

I'm disappointed with the city, I have to say. It's very large, but there's nothing left of the Pharaonic times, not even of the later Roman or Greek times, and nothing of the Byzantine times to note. There's nothing romantic about the city of Alexandria except its name and the sea. Its name I associate with the novel series, *The Alexandria Quartet*, but it's a big, sprawling, third-world city with large high-rises. Apparently, many of them are used by vacationers in the summertime. Here it's breezier and the temperatures are lower than in the interior of the country, so a large number of Egyptians come here several months of the year.

I'm just getting over jet lag now. During the long days, when my host is attending conferences, I'm taking walks along the boardwalk. I met my first Egyptian today, that is, the first Egyptian I've met spontaneously, without planning, and he turned out to be a Copt. His name is Victor. He saw me looking out over the sea and he asked me if I'm an American. When he discovered that I speak English, he began at once to practice his English with me at some great length, following me along the boardwalk. Finally, he prevailed upon me to visit his widowed mother. He lives with her some blocks away. We had tea. She doesn't speak any English at all, but spoke French, so we carried on something of a rough-hewn conversation. Victor and his mother are not only Coptic; they are also Catholic. Victor told me that there are many Catholics in Alexandria, and that Alexandria still retains something of a more international, or at least a trans-Mediterranean, character. But south of Alexandria, Egypt becomes progressively more and more Islamic all the way into Cairo. Then south of Cairo, the number of Copts begins to increase again.

## *Of Sand Castles and Christian Churches*

SEPTEMBER 4, THURSDAY

I built a little sand castle on a nearby beach today and, intriguingly, some boys who came by—fourteen, fifteen, sixteen years old—watched me with great interest. Apparently, they didn't think that building sand castles is a typical activity for people to do on the beach, and when I looked around, I noticed that no one else was making them. Maybe it's something that only Americans or Europeans do. The boys watched with interest until one of them became very disturbed and exclaimed in Arabic, "*el kanessa,*" a church! I wasn't dressed like a priest; I was dressed very informally for making a sand castle on the beach. Yet the boy thought that the castle was a church and accused me of trying to spread Christianity in Egypt by building a representation of Christian churches! I was *very* surprised.

Without their knowing anything about my being a Catholic priest, I had been "discovered," as it were. The first person I met was a Catholic Copt who asked me very quickly if I am also a Catholic. The second encounter I had was with Muslim boys who accused me of trying to build a church. So it's really an interesting place of discovery for me: seeing the character of these people and how deeply their religious concerns and issues preoccupy them and how they tend to interpret everything they experience through the prism of their faith. In seconds, the boys kicked down the towers of my castle and ran away...triumphant, or afraid?

I note that my skills in speaking Arabic are less than I had hoped for. The classical Arabic of my last year of study in the States is not at all the colloquial form spoken by everyone here!

## A Stranger in Cairo

### September 5, Friday

I took the train today from Alexandria to Cairo and arrived in the afternoon, very hot, with all my bags. There was no one to meet me at the train station in Cairo. I have no contacts here. No one from the patriarchal office nor any of the people to whom I wrote at the University of Cairo ever responded to my letters. So here I am in a strange city, barely speaking the language, without knowing anyone at all. It's chaos out there. Well, I'm sure it's not chaos, but to an American accustomed to other kinds of urban organization, it seems impossible to negotiate.

I finally got into a taxi. It seems to me that the taxi driver actually appropriated me; he grabbed me and all my bags. He asked me where I wanted to go and I asked his advice. He looked over my general demeanor, my clothing, and my bags. He took me to the Shepherd Hotel (an old English hotel from the nineteenth-century time of English governmental occupation) and I checked in.

### September 6, Saturday

The Shepherd Hotel is quite nice. Yesterday evening I met a lovely German couple. I traveled around with them a little bit today, an elderly couple. Like good Germans who are always very well-studied travelers, they had done research in their guide books prior to their trip so that they could get more out of each moment of their tour. Very frugal, as I always imagine German travelers to be, and very opinionated. Lots of interesting discussions which, unfortunately, reflected a very weak but intensely believed form of Christianity which they shared with me at great length as well.

I left them this morning, and now must begin to make my way to the patriarchal headquarters in Cairo to set up my monastery stay. At the same time, I must try to get the monies I wired here from the States.

## Missing Funds

When I went to the bank to withdraw some of the funds I had sent here, I met a problem. Bank Misr (Misr = Egypt) is not far from the Shepherd Hotel. I walked in and went up to a clerk. After identifying myself, I showed him the letter indicating that I had wired the money. The clerk disappeared for a while and then came back with the manager. He asked, "To what particular Bank Misr did you wire it?"

I responded that I didn't know. I had simply wired it to Bank Misr; since it is the national bank, I had assumed that it was automated and that you would be able to tap into its computer to locate the particular account into which the money had been deposited. He smiled and said that the banks in Egypt are not fully automated and that there is no computer linkage among all the Bank Misrs. Although they are formally one organization, they are not coordinated electronically. So, without knowing which particular bank the wire went to, he couldn't give me any of that money.

"How can I discover which Bank Misr it was?" I asked.

"You go to each one of them and ask, 'Is this the bank that has this account?'"

"How many Bank Misrs are there?"

"Oh," he answered, "there are several hundred across Egypt!" So this leaves me in a very difficult position. Several thousands of dollars—all that I need for my whole year of fieldwork in Egypt— is in that bank somewhere, but I don't know how to get it. I have forty or fifty dollars in my pocket and that's it. I have a few checks left from my academic budget, but without a bank account, how can I cash them?

So I'm going to check out of this hotel tomorrow morning and go to some place far cheaper. That is very possible, judging from what I saw when I was riding in the taxi. Then I'm going to make my way quickly to a monastery to do my living and working there. I must also try to find someone who can help me obtain the funds which were wired here.


SEPTEMBER 7, SUNDAY

I checked into the Talat Harb Hotel today. Really the hotel of the third-world traveler. But it's fifty cents a day; that's the incredible thing! Even with my very meager funds, I can handle staying here for some time, though I hazard to describe the conditions of this hotel, even in my notes. Suffice it to say that it's neither sanitary nor safe, and there are lots of people staying here from all sides of life, people I might otherwise not get to meet, and from places all around the world to which I might never get to go. Sudanese refugees; Ethiopian deportees; Ugandan expatriates; failed college students; unemployed Lebanese migrants; and some very intense-looking Islamic religious devotees. But here I will stay until I find out what else I can do.

> *Father of Glory,*
> *What else can I be, but exultant? So rarely can I exercise fair trust in your Providence as now. Now I reap the consequence of my own carelessness. What have I done? I have come thousands of miles into a world utterly foreign to me, with fearful aspects for me in my ignorance. The language I studied is really not the one these people speak, and the contacts upon which I had depended have dried up or disappeared. My return ticket is dated for months away, and I am loath to attempt to reschedule my homecoming, preferring to be lost to the world than to be a complete failure in it. My grant and virtually all my funds are lost in a hopeless maze of Arab bureaucracy, and I am residing in squalor.*
> *I am completely exhausted. If I collapse, as is likely, I shall at last know this side of the Cross and come to know Jesus as have his finer friends. If I somehow recover beforehand, or thereafter, I shall have a testimony of your power and kindness by which I could encourage others. I feel the joy of falling into*

*your hands—as much or more by the accumulation of my faults as by the lot drawn for me. And although you would be just in dropping me further into the pit toward which I am headed, I have my whole attention turned to the moment of my reception into your hands, rather than on what may happen afterward.*

*I thank you heartily for the drama of this hour. How else could I better commit my faith in your forgiveness of my faults and the upholding of your love? The grace of this moment is better than any success which may follow, and offsets in value any failures I may suffer. St. Ignatius prayed, "Give me only Thy love and Thy grace." I understand better now the meaning of the next line, "then do with me what Thou wilt." Thank you for the lightness of faith in the gravity of life. In spite of my weakness, I feel glad enough to think: "If these be all the kinds of reversals and oppositions I will face in the rest of my life, I would shortly be the saint I have always failed to be till now." The Cross he bids me take up today is the "sweet yoke" and "light burden" he promised, so I pray this in his name, Christ Jesus, my Lord.*

## All Things Egyptian

SEPTEMBER 8, MONDAY

It was a very tiring day. The heat in Cairo is still terrible. It's hard to get around this city, and one gets to be pretty soiled very early in the effort to negotiate it. Traffic is extraordinarily congested and quite lawless to my eyes. At any rate, I tried to make my way to the Patriarchate today to see Pope Shenouda, hoping that he had received my several letters, though he has never answered any of them. Getting there was quite a project. I'm becoming very reluctant to part with any funds. Paying taxis is an art in Cairo. The drivers recognize a tourist, especially an American, and rates seem to go up. I'm having to learn how to negotiate with them by naming a price stiffly and assertively when I first get in, and not deviating from it. If I don't name a price and let them name it, by the time I get out, the fare will be too high. But I find that I can walk, and it's good exercise. I'm getting over jet lag now altogether and getting into the swing of things here, surrendering myself to the vicissitudes of life in this city and in this country.

I'm also eating the food that the Egyptians eat, no longer feeling that I can afford to eat in hotels or restaurants where tourists go, as they are much more expensive. There are plenty of small shops that sell a bean-and-bread combination called *fule wa tamaya* which is very tasty, especially if they put some spices and herbs on it. I remember how the Hebrews were longing for the leeks and garlic of Egypt when they were in Sinai, and now I know why. There are plenty of good spices here, which people add to a sandwich-like affair on pita bread. They also make very good juices here from fruit they crush in a hand press to mix in a delicious concoction. The very thing I was told by the travelogues *not* to drink, the very food I was advised *not* to eat because I could get sick from it, I have surrendered myself to eating and to drinking. Otherwise, it would be a very difficult year, not to mention a pricey one. My only option is to live as the natives do, which, of course, is what anthropologists are required to do.

## A Fruitless Trip

SEPTEMBER 9, TUESDAY

After asking a lot of directions and walking a very long way (it seems halfway across the city), I arrived at the Patriarchate only to discover that Pope Shenouda is not in today. I was told I should try to make an appointment, but that it may take a couple of days to negotiate! (The Western reader should note that the title "Pope" is as ancient a title of the Coptic Patriarch as the Roman Catholic one; likewise, both prelates are called "His Holiness.") I was intending to solve the problem of my placement in a monastery by dealing with lower ecclesiastical officials, but virtually everybody here insists that I will have to see the Pope! But as is the case in very centralized institutions, access to the central office here is difficult.

I had to sit and wait and talk to a whole series of secretaries. Most of them are lay women; one or two of them are clerics. They told me to come back tomorrow and continue waiting and that they would do what they could to arrange a meeting. I gather nothing here is going to be set in stone in terms of scheduling. This is something I'm just going to have to negotiate day by day.

## *A Beggar among Beggars*

There's a beautiful—well, almost beautiful—cathedral here called St. Mark's Cathedral which I'm told is the largest church in Africa. The relics of St. Mark were brought back from Venice and are entombed below. The building is finished only on the outside. The inside is filled with scaffolding, and although liturgies are sometimes celebrated here, it is by no means a fully decorated or a fully furnished church. Even so, I understand that it is already used for the Pope's larger ceremonies.

There are many beggars on the steps of this church, on the steps of the papal residence, and on the steps of what might be considered the curia offices of Pope Shenouda. All of them ask for alms, especially from visiting clergy. I'm dressed in clerics now to visit the Pope so they can see that I'm a visiting priest. They know how to ask for money in English and in any number of other languages but, unfortunately, I have none to give them.

I was happy to see that one very old priest sits at the door of a small chapel near the great Cathedral of St. Mark. He breaks off pieces of bread and gives them to everyone who comes into the gate of the shrine. So, if I make two or three visits, I'll have enough for tomorrow's breakfast!

## *Watching and Waiting*

SEPTEMBER 10, WEDNESDAY

I suppose there's nothing new to report. I've been making my way now from the Talat Harb Hotel to the Patriarchate the last couple of days and doing what I did the first time I arrived there: simply waiting. I wait from relatively early in the morning, 9:30 A.M. or 10:00 A.M., all the way till late in the evening, to 6:00 P.M. or 7:00 P.M.

No one can tell me for sure if, or when, the Pope will see me, or if I'll be able to meet with anyone who might be able to help me coordinate a visit to the monasteries. I have spoken with several of the secretaries as I have waited, hopefully not too impatiently, telling them that it isn't necessary for me to see the Pope; it was only suggested to me by a Coptic associate I met in New York, and that I would be perfectly happy to get to the monastery by any means whatever. But everyone here seems to think that something like this must be arranged through the Pope himself.

I'm becoming familiar with many of the secretaries and the staff who work in the papal curia in Cairo. Now they're beginning to bring me bottles of Coca-Cola, little snack candies and chocolates, and they all want to practice their English. It's a real fixation among the young, especially. Apparently they realize that there are economic opportunities which will become available to them to the degree that they can master this important language of commerce. They also ask me about their relatives who have gone to America, in case I might at least know something about the places to which they've gone.

So, one by one, they trickle in to see me. I'm beginning to have guests as if I were a special legate to the Coptic Church! People come in and ask me questions. They're curious about what I'm doing here, but they're more interested in exploring the English language with me. I'm happy to oblige, as I have absolutely nothing else to do and it's a way of making some informal contacts.

### Surprise!

September 11, Thursday

Today in the Talat Harb Hotel, I found a Romanian gentleman sleeping in my room! They're doubling people up, apparently, without asking! Poor man, he's trying to get to Italy instead of going back to Romania when his state-sponsored engineering job in Egypt is finished. I listened to him complain, then cry, about the misery of his life in Romania, and found myself writing a check which emptied out my entire academic budget. It was a check for only a couple of hundred dollars, which I probably would have had trouble cashing here anyway, since I have no local bank account. But he has an account somewhere and feels that he can buy his ticket and visa now. And so I pray:

> *Merciful Father,*
> *You saw the affliction of your people in slavery and you heard their cry. As slaves and children of slaves, they no longer remembered your name, nor were the gods of their enslavers theirs to invoke. They were born into misery and they*

*labored without rest or reward till they died without rites. Only the names of the tribes from which they came remained with them, the bloodlines of their tragic heritage, for they were still given in marriage, and still they extended their fathers' lineages. This was an act of hope, a virtue of the Covenant you had made with Abraham so long before, but that had been otherwise forgotten.*

*All this befell them here in Egypt, and here, till now, your other children languish as before. You said to Abraham, "I will bless those who bless you." So I say, "Blessed be Abraham," and bless this poor man who seeks my help. To the prophet, you spoke, "Blessed be my people, Egypt." Make it come to pass, this word which was true when you first spoke it, for they have sunk low into poverty and desperation. Blessed be the Moslem, the Christian, the Jew! Show your Face of Mercy—to all of us here.*

*And I, in the House of Jesus, who know of Abraham only because of his sacrifice in yielding up Isaac, I bless Jesus' Name and his holy lineage from Abraham. I bless Jesus' sojourn in Egypt where he was hosted as a child. By Abraham's friendship with you, call down your blessing on this poor soul who has too little known your help.*

*Oh, what ruin has been visited on his people! They labor, too, as slaves in Eastern Europe under a yoke twice as bitter, because no names either of yours or of their cultural lineages may be invoked. They marry little and bear young less in loveless days. In crowded, darkened cities they huddle, their former churches gutted and their hearts cold. Bring it down, this terrible slavery! Make it go, uproot it forever! You who have always hated slavery, liberate them there and tell them your Name. Make them yours again or, better still, make them yours as never before.*

*But this poor man here, let him sleep a little and forget much. And when you wake him, let some secret seed of grace take root and give him hope. Once, as a baby, he was loved, or at least he believed it enough to risk living and growing older. Now, reconfirm that original hope by a new faith in your Providence. May he even see his sufferings as a sign of a great sacrifice, to be joined to the Covenant of Abraham and Isaac, Christ and his Cross. For this I pray in his Name. Amen.*

## *A Fateful Audience*

SEPTEMBER 12, FRIDAY

Well, it seemed like today would be yet another wasted day waiting in the Patriarchate of Cairo. It's something I would not ordinarily be willing to do, I suppose, except that being rather penniless, waiting around in Cairo, being fed occasional Coca-Colas and candies, it is about the best thing I can do. And perhaps, like the beggars on the doorstep, I may eventually become such a nuisance that they'll have to remedy the problem that I represent.

But today, finally, toward the end of the day there was a little breakthrough. It came about through the secretaries: these women who are running back and forth, doing all the paper work and answering all the telephones. They have seen me waiting here these last three or four days and have become progressively more and more agitated on my account. They have been speaking more and more sharply to the higher clergy whose offices they serve.

Finally, today, two of them double-teamed the bishop who is in charge of the Pope's appointments. One went in, and then the other one went in, independently of each other. Then both of them went in together and I even heard raised voices. I'm not sure that I understood everything, but I did hear something about respect and hospitality, or something to that effect. I'm sure they were arguing that I'm entitled by now, that I've *earned* the right to see the Pope simply by the wholesale loss of the greater part of this week waiting for him.

So eventually, the bishop came out, Anba Serapion, the Bishop of Ecumenical Affairs, one of the more important secretaries of the Pope. He walked me over to the papal residence which is just across a driveway from the curia offices. We went up a set of stairs into a beautiful lobby area and in just a few minutes I was taken in to see his Holiness, Pope Shenouda III. He was sitting at the end of a long table with high-backed chairs. He greeted me very warmly. He embraced me, kissed me on both cheeks, and sat me down. I spoke to him about the letters I had written. He nodded his head, acknowledging neither that he remembered them nor that he didn't get them. He just listened to what I had to say. Since I didn't know how much he was apprised of my intentions, I reviewed them briefly with him in about five or ten minutes. I told

*His Holiness Pope Shenoudah the Third.*

him of my desire to do anthropological study, offered him all my respect, assured him of my carefulness in doing the work, and asked for access to the monasteries.

He looked at me and paused a moment and finally said, "Could you grow a beard?" Then he asked, "Do you have a religious habit?" These were his "requirements." He didn't say they were but, by the tone of his voice, these seemed to be his two requirements: that I grow a beard and wear a religious habit. I presume it was his intent that I would not be uncomfortable myself, nor would I make anyone else uncomfortable by the way I presented myself. So I assured him that I have a religious habit and that I would wear it in the monasteries if I had his permission to do so. He laughed at the idea that he needed to give me, a Catholic monk, permission to wear my religious habit. He thanked me—actually a polite order—for wearing it from now on, whether in Cairo or anywhere else in Egypt, and for making it the *only* garb that I would wear. And he also told me that, from here on, I was not to shave, because it is inappropriate for monks to be clean-shaven. Whether that be the Western custom or not, it's not something Egyptians are familiar with, or appreciative of, in a monk.

Those were his big interests. My philosophical point of view, my social science point of view, or my theological point of view—none of these seemed to be particularly important to him. But after we had come to terms on these two points, he proceeded to take out some beautiful stationery bearing his insignia, and wrote me a letter. Well, actually, he wrote a letter for me to carry, to present to any of the heads of the monasteries which I will visit. In a beautiful script, in cursive Arabic characters, Pope Shenouda wrote:

To the Heads of all the Monasteries of Egypt, and to their Leading Officials:
Grace and Peace from your Father and Brother.

This letter introduces Mark Gruber, a monk and priest from one of the Catholic monasteries of America. He desires to study in our monasteries. Please receive him some days in your monastery, and make available to him all that he needs for his work.

I am sure that he will find his sojourn among us enriching both spiritually and culturally.

Shenouda III

He drew a cross on top of the page and wrote the date on the bottom. Then he showed the letter to me and asked me to read it back to him. When I hesitated to do so, he helped me to understand it. After clearing that, he gave me a list of the monasteries he expects me to visit, one at a time, first, second, third. St. Macarius he wishes me to visit first, and then St. Bishoi where he wishes me to spend most of my time. "In St. Macarius," he said, "you will stay long enough to grow a beard, and then you will go to St. Bishoi Monastery." This is the monastery in which the Pope spends every weekend of his pontificate on retreat. "You will go to that monastery for the longest amount of time during your stay in Egypt. After you have finished the liturgical cycles of Advent, Lent, and Easter, then you will travel during the remainder of your field trip to the other monasteries in Upper Egypt and in the Eastern Desert."

After outlining my itinerary, he presented me with a box of chocolates. I didn't know whether I was supposed to eat any or not so when he took one out of the box and put it into my hand, I interpreted this as a sign that it was not impolite to eat chocolate in front of the Pope, so I did. He seemed to be very happy that I liked it. In fact, I did like it. Since I had eaten less that I might have ordinarily eaten in the last few days, the chocolate was quite good.

After I left the papal residence, his secretary (in this case, a layman who didn't speak English) ran after me to tell me that I needed to come back to the papal residence on Tuesday morning when a special driver would be provided to take me to St. Macarius Monastery.

### *The Next Step on the Journey*

SEPTEMBER 16, TUESDAY

I came, then, to the residence of the Pope this morning, and was met by a gentleman and his wife and child who were making a pilgrimage to St. Macarius Monastery. They were excited to be going there, and were very pleased to be able to take me. They had been asked by the secretary of the Pope to drive me there. I was surprised that one could simply drive to such a remote monastery, but they said that in the last few years the access roads off the so-called "desert highway" between Cairo and Alexandria were clear enough and smooth enough to allow conventional vehicles to travel to these monasteries.

So we made our way. But, within a mile or two of the monastery, the jeep broke down and we had to walk the remaining mile or mile and a half on foot, carrying our bags. I was quite pleased about that because, really, that was an opportunity to come to the monastery more like a pilgrim than like a tourist: a little bit tired, a little bit dusty from the desert, a little bit chastened by the severity of its heat and its dryness.

### The Desert of the Wadi Natroun

We eventually arrived at the Monastery of St. Macarius. It's a beautiful place, much better than I thought the monasteries of Egypt would be. My driver explained that this is, perhaps, the most refined monastic setting in Egypt owing to the fact that its current abbot, Abuna Matta el Meskeen, Matthew the Poor, is a rather visionary fellow who is progressive in terms of his concept of monastic routine, monastic architecture, and monastic holiness and spirituality. The monastery is simply better organized and cleaner, he said. The driver told me that the melons which are grown in the walled farm of this particular monastery—which is really much more than the traditional enclosed garden of an earlier epoch, actually a great farm—are the sweetest melons which supply most of the best hotels in Cairo.

There are hundreds of laymen here who are the employees of the monastery. The monks themselves are also very busy providing all of the various services of the monastery. Their jobs range from working on the farm, to the machine shop, to the printing presses, to cleaning and custodial work, to supervising personnel, to providing spiritual direction and offering prayers for those who have come in need of them: a lot of activities. Some of the monks are also summoned to go out regularly to help in parishes where there are no priests either in Alexandria or in Cairo, or even in the Delta where they can travel more readily using the desert highway.

When I arrived here, the guest-master priest, Abuna Zachariah, showed me a beautiful cell with a sitting room, a kitchenette, a room for prayer, and a small chamber with a bed. Not very bad at all, modest but comfortable; a very prayerful and quiet place.

*Blessed Lord,*

*You brought me at last to the open desert today! All my senses are overwhelmed! Without trees and hills, clouds or buildings, no shadows diminish the brilliance of the noonday sun. My eyes squint from the strain. No trees or leaves catch the wind, so it moves with force, but almost soundlessly, except for the low drone of gusts sweeping up from the surface, or the dull brush of air against my ears. The heat baked through my black habit and drew away all perspiration through the fabric, leaving me dry. Tonight the temperature dropped fast as the sun set, and I was delighted by the cool breezes. I have never seen such stars as under the night sky here. No city lights in any distance, no sounds from the streets. The world I have known is far away, and I am at last as alone as I ever hoped to be.*

*In my aloneness, in the purest solitude, you are achingly present. Yet, in the silence of the desert night, I hear the muffled voices of "the poor, banished children of Eve" calling out to you from every place. A deafening din of pain and guilt, of need and grief rises up, and in the soundless vastness I can hear the echoes of the cries that pierce the heavens. Never have I wanted to pray as I do here. Never have I wanted to intercede so much. From my own soul, I hear groans and sighs, and all sorts of intimations of joy which well up with the impulse of your Spirit to pray.*

*Is this why Moses told Pharaoh that you required him to take his people on "a three days' journey into the desert"? Did you await from them there the Covenant-prescribed sacrifices which would renew and confirm Israel and bring them, at last, out of their slavery?*

### The Controversial Letter

SEPTEMBER 17, WEDNESDAY

I will not get much fieldwork done here. The monks are reticent to talk to me and I have slowly become aware of the fact that there is some hesitation to dialogue with me precisely *because* of this letter that I carry from Pope Shenouda. This particular monastery, or at least the head of this monastery and, perhaps by extension, its members, are living in some tension with the Pope. Apparently,

Abuna Matta el Meskeen is a rather charismatic figure who has taken some exception to the policies of Pope Shenouda in the practical running of the Coptic Church. He has criticized the Pope in public on some occasions and, therefore, there is something of a rift between them. My coming here with a letter from Pope Shenouda asking for hospitality on his account might not have been the most promising entrée into the fellowship of these monks.

Nevertheless, this is where Pope Shenouda told me to go first, to settle into first, "for so long as it takes you to grow a respectable beard." I expect this will be about two and a half weeks or so. How wonderful that Pope Shenouda would send me to visit the monastery at some variance with himself, and that he could count on their hospitality for his own guest! All Churches have such conflicts, but not all leaders are so gracious.

## A Dissertation of Blank Pages

SEPTEMBER 20, SATURDAY

Today I discreetly chastened the brother who brought food to my door. "Why won't you talk with me? I have a great deal to learn if I am to understand your life!" He answered, almost as a reflex, "You will understand us best if you bear our silence. Silence reveals us more than words." I sigh. It may be true, as he says, but a dissertation of blank pages will only win me an invisible doctorate!

Nevertheless, a failed doctoral project reveals the mystery of the Paschal Sacrifice which is at the heart of the monastic vocation and the essential matter of my investigation. If I obtain enough material for a thesis, I win, because I will have found the facts and explained them in terms of the symbolic unity of the Copts' spirituality and culture. If I fail to do so, I also win, because the symbolic weight of sacrifice spent without guarantees of success is my personal lesson, perfectly learned.

## A Roman Liturgy

SEPTEMBER 25, THURSDAY

A surprise, after ten days of relative isolation: today several of the younger monks, uncharacteristically, given their shyness, solitude, and silence, approached me and asked if they might attend a Mass that I was celebrating. I have been praying the Mass privately inasmuch as I am a Roman Catholic and the monks are Orthodox, so I am unable to receive Communion with them. I have been saying my Mass in the prayer room of the cell they gave me. The young monks invited me to have Mass in the *hesn*, or keep, in the fortress area of the monastery in which there are some auxiliary altars. I willingly obliged them. I prepared an altar inside the fortress and, in the late morning, I celebrated a Catholic Mass which they observed.

Because I know that they are accustomed to a rather long and protracted Liturgy, I attempted to give the Roman ritual a little more elaboration than it ordinarily enjoys. I sang most of the Mass parts, all the orations and the Penitential Rite; I sang the Gloria and the Credo. I decided to add the Sequence of Pentecost and the Litany of Saints near the Petitions, which I sang as well. I sang the Eucharistic Canon; I sang a series of devotional hymns, including the *Salve Regina*, after Communion. All told, the Mass lasted an hour and a half or an hour and forty-five minutes.

When I finished, the brothers were very grateful, congratulating me for being able to provide what they considered to be a beautiful Liturgy. But I shall never forget that one of them exclaimed to me how he was just beginning to enter into the spirit of the Mass when it was over! "Such a short Mass," he said, "that you celebrate in the West." What an extraordinary idea! The longest possible Mass I could have said was for him a short Mass. Indeed, how completely different is this mentality from that of the West! There, people are chained to the fetters of the watch around their wrist and are constantly consulting it, even during the most sacred moments of the Mass. By constantly checking this "ball and chain" around their wrist, they are deprived of the freedom to enjoy the blessings of worship, and are confined to the slavery of work and routine and schedules.

## Postscript

### SEPTEMBER 30, TUESDAY

Outside of Egypt, St. Macarius is perhaps the best known Coptic monastery. As already noted, its abbot, Abuna Matta el Meskeen, Matthew the Poor, is widely published and translated. I became familiar with the dramatic narrative frequently told about this monastery among the Copts themselves, and although it admits of glosses which could use historical refinements, the story stands as a piece of contemporary hagiography, part of the living heritage of the monks who live here.

It was once, and for centuries, the greatest and most populous monastery in Egypt. But with the shifting fortunes of the Coptic Church, St. Macarius slowly declined through time until, by the 1960s, it nearly dissolved. However, in a dramatic moment associated with Holy Week services, the monastery was rescued by an influx of new young monks. Under the charismatic leadership of Abuna Matta el Meskeen, they restored the venerable House almost at once to its prominent role at the center of Coptic spiritual life and monastic institutions.

# OCTOBER
## A TIME OF NEW BEGINNINGS

### *The Pope's Monastery*

OCTOBER 1, WEDNESDAY

Today I arrived at the Monastery of St. Bishoi. I was driven here by one of the pilgrims who is making a tour of the monasteries of the Wadi Natroun. The monasteries in this particular region are very close to each other, so it was only a matter of twenty minutes' or half an hour's drive from one house to the other.

### *A Fateful Encounter*

After I had left the car and had started walking toward the monastery, I noticed that, at some distance away, a group of monks were all gathered around an old monk whom they were assisting, almost carrying, through the door of the monastery. I walked slowly in that direction and entered shortly after they did. To me, the monks seemed to be escorting the aged monk into the monastery, almost as if it were his homecoming. Or had he, perhaps, become faint as he attempted to walk in the hot desert sun? In any case, his entry amid the throng at the moment of my arrival seemed propitious.

Apparently this monk, Abuna Elia, had been living in a cave for many years—for ten or eleven years, if I'm not mistaken—and had hardly been seen during all of that time. But when the monks discovered that he was ill and thought that he should no longer live alone as a hermit in the cave, they escorted him back to St. Bishoi. I gather he was highly reluctant to come, but they had prepared a cell for him and they were promising him that he would not be disturbed, that he could live in great silence.

When he saw me entering through the deep, low door of the ancient wall, the others with him also observed me, so I created a further commotion in addition to the stir he was creating. He turned to me and said, "You are a Roman." In English, he said it.

"Yes," I responded. I was wearing my Benedictine habit. I hadn't realized that any monk here would recognize it as a "Roman" habit.

He said, "Then, you will want to see me; you will want to have some opportunity to talk with me," he said in English again. "Yes, Abuna," I said, "I would be very happy to see you."

Somehow, I feel that this old monk believes that our coming to the gate of the monastery at the same moment has some significance and, therefore, he is open to speak with me for whatever reason he imagines that God might have for so conjoining our arrival.


OCTOBER 3, FRIDAY

> *Gentle Jesus,*
>
> *Although they are very gracious, I think that some of the monks here are afraid of me, or at least apprehensive. A monk, they understand; an American, they have sure opinions about; but an American monk is not a concept they can easily grasp. (Maybe we don't quite grasp it either.) I am giving up the additional task of explaining the paradox of the priest and anthropologist to them just now. Help me just to rest in their presence, not minding the awkwardness of their hesitations. Let me not so focus upon their discomfort as to signal my own apprehension, and worsen matters.*
>
> *Thank you for Abuna Zachariah, who pulled my hood over my head before I left St. Macarius Monastery saying, "You can wear this." Thank you for his concern to provide me with better decorum so that I could be integrated more easily here. Let my hood be a sign of my resting under the cover of your palm. Let it be a sign that your hand is on me too, and that your authority is strong enough to subordinate all the*

*contradictions they fear in me and I fear in myself. Thank you for the blessed relief throughout these days of simple fare and sparse meals. How glad my body feels to have no place to go to seek gratification, other than to stand before you in peace!*

## Becoming Acclimated

OCTOBER 5, SUNDAY

During these days I am becoming immersed in the monastic routine, entering as much as possible into the schedules of prayers, both communal and private, that the monks have adopted.

Both in St. Macarius and in St. Bishoi Monastery, the monks rise very early in the morning. Here they arise at 2:30 A.M. and begin prayer at 3:00 A.M. Morning Prayer consists of more than seventy psalms which are sung, one after the other, with various antiphons, short hymns, intercessions, and incensations from 3:00 A.M. until 6:00 A.M.—all of this done while standing! Then, at 6:00 A.M. the Coptic Mass (the Kodes) begins and continues till long past 9:00 A.M. or 9:30 A.M.

So, in fact, the monks have six hours of standing in a very thick cloud of incense every morning before they can even have their first glass of tea! This is the routine from which they never deviate; this is the routine which is the rhythm of their life, and it is exhausting. Nevertheless, it is also very moving, and the manner in which the monks celebrate these prayers is altogether genuine and sincere—nothing affected, no sense of drudgery, either. It's their work, their primary work, but it's a work which they perform with great sincerity, great veneration, and great reverence in an almost simple, childlike way.

The monks complete the whole Psalter in the course of the day (150 Psalms in Coptic or Arabic!), which is an extraordinary number. It takes a certain amount of practice and determination to enter into this regime. The Rule of St. Benedict provides for 150 psalms a week (with certain repetitions and canticles), whereas in my own Benedictine Abbey, we cover the same number in a month! We pray them much more slowly and with pauses, but we are seated. Comparisons are difficult.

OCTOBER 7, TUESDAY

I have been trying to master some of the linguistic aspects of life here: the proper responses during the Kodes and Office, and the proper answers to prayers. I am trying to write them down and to rehearse them. There are any number of monks here who are good at teaching this. I am just familiarizing myself with life in the monastery as much as possible so that I can be, if not a competent participant, at least one not so incompetent as to be jarring and disturbing for those among whom I am living and praying. I hope that by this sign of good intention and zeal to enter into their common prayer life I will also give the monks occasion to be more receptive to me and more forthcoming regarding the questions I ask and the needs I have.

In the meantime, I am getting used to the monastic diet. It is more or less the same here as it was in St. Macarius: the *felafel* bean with rice and tea—hot tea by the glass—always. Everyone always wants to put far too much sugar in it. The monks look at me quizzically when I say, "No sugar." I'm becoming reluctant to say "No sugar" anymore, and I'm beginning to permit at least one spoonful, when I note that the monks are putting four or five tablespoons of sugar into their tea! The tea, the rice, and the beans, as well as the coarse bread, which is very delicious, are the common diet here. On occasion, there are slices of tomato or slices of cucumber to go with it. A very simple diet, but very tasty, even though it's repeated twice a day. But what will they do when they have a feast?

## Blessings from a Cave-Dweller

OCTOBER 10, FRIDAY

When I made the day-long walk to Deir el Baramous, the abbot of the monastery informed me that I should seek a blessing from an elderly monk who has been living in a nearby cave for the last several years. "Pilgrims," he said, "should seek blessings."

So I was escorted to the mouth of the cave and waited for the desert monk to appear. He comes out every few days to pick up the portion of food which the monks leave for him. He came out and, following my nearly liturgical instructions, I grabbed him by the ankle and said, "Pray, Abuna, a blessing." He said to me—with the dramatic effect of my hearing his word, which seemed to break years of monastic silence—"Our Faith is easy and simple, as simple as the alphabet."

Startled, I let go of his ankle. He re-entered the cave and I walked back to Deir el Baramous, contemplating this strange word I had received. I stayed there that night.

## The Alphabet of Faith

OCTOBER 13, MONDAY

After returning to Deir St. Bishoi the next day, I continued to ponder the old monk's words. I decided that I hadn't fully understood his message, so I walked back to the cave again today and called in to the old man. "I don't understand what you said, Abuna. What do you mean, 'Our Faith is as easy, as simple as the alphabet'?"

Coming out of the cave, the old monk said, "In the ancient tongue, *alpha* means 'eagle.' It is the bird of heaven, that which represents God—transcendent, over all. *Beta* is the Hebrew word; we hear it in the name 'Bethel.' It means 'house, home,' the place in which we are familiar, comfortable, in control, the place where we live out our lives day to day. But these two words, so opposite, have been conjoined: 'alpha' and 'beta,' because in Christ Jesus, heaven is wedded to earth. Christ is the Word made flesh to dwell among us, to pitch his tent in our midst. We are not estranged any longer. This is easy; this is simple," the old monk said. "Every child knows the alphabet, and so can any heart accept our Faith."

Back at St. Bishoi, Abuna Sidrak told me a similar account about the "alphabet" when I asked him about it, so this idea is widely circulated here! I much enjoy this manner of life in which I may hike about, seeking good words, and then return "home" to dialogue with the monks about what they mean. But this is exactly what the Desert Fathers did, as recorded in the literature I read long ago.

OCTOBER 16, THURSDAY

*O Great and Silent God,*
*You spoke once and it came to be. You speak now and all things perdure; they arise and proceed toward their goal. Once*

*your Word became flesh to dwell among us. Now our flesh is nourished by your Word, and your flesh is our very food. You are speaking; your word fills the world and covers all flesh. Life quickens in the womb at your word, and the dead are awakened when you call their names. The breath of a "word" from your mouth was rolled into clay, and our very flesh was held in your hands. The bread in our hands is blessed by your Word, and your flesh is provided to seal our union with you.*

*Blessed may you be who gave us the ears of our heart to hear you! Before our tongues can speak, we are able to hear and to ponder. Blessed may you be who stills every voice and quiets all earthly tumult till your word pierces the heavens and reaches us. And blessed may you be forever whose silent, eternal discourse of love within the mystery of your one un-speakable Name has become a Word of revelation in our hear-ing, and a message of salvation before our eyes.*

*Thank you for giving me the grace of contemplating your silence at this moment in my life. Here, in this place without boundaries and barriers, walls or roads, signs or properties, I hear nothing. I see only the featureless, open expanse of space, and at length I see nothing. Blessed may you be whose silence in the nothingness of uncreated grace has become my medita-tion, that as I continually transcend the words and things of my life, I can find you in the purity of this desert retreat.*

### *An American Spy?*

OCTOBER 19, SUNDAY

Pilgrims passing through today pressed me for the reason for my presence here. After a lengthy explanation, which I thought was clear enough, I heard the father of the visiting family sum it all up in the English word: SPY!

Yikes! That was *not* my meaning. I must shore up the pilgrim-age aspect of this sojourn, or I shall get nowhere. And, come to think of it, why should I do otherwise? Always, I am thrown back to considering that God has done intensive anthropological field-work by the Incarnation of his Son. He did so not to spy on us, but rather, by the pilgrimage, the *transitus*, the exodus of his Cross to permanently abide with us, and we in him.

Will my heart remain here long years from now, if I regard my visitation as a pilgrimage? I suspect so already. Did not the heart of Jesus remain among the people with whom he sojourned?

## A Babel of Languages

OCTOBER 25, SATURDAY

Languages are blurring! I am memorizing Coptic prayers and hymns from the monastery's worship. These words are evoking the memories of my old Greek classes, stirring up the dust of ecclesiastical Latin, and sending me into linguistic confusion. Of all things, I am spontaneously using German words in my rare conversations, realizing, I suppose with some frustration, the limits of my Arabic. I am getting headaches from it all! I am glad all over again that the Word became flesh to dwell among us. Otherwise, on the word level alone, we would surely fail to grasp the weight and value of his communication!

## Midnight Prayer of the Third Watch

OCTOBER 31, FRIDAY

The desert monk prays:

"With eyes full of compassion, O Lord, look upon my weakness, for life is well nigh to its end, and in my works there is no salvation. Wherefore, I beseech Thee, O Lord, look upon my weakness, my affliction, my lowliness and my sojourning with merciful eyes and save me."

*Holy Lord,*
*How humbly these monks find themselves in your Presence! All day and all night they worship you, ponder you in silence, read of you, and long for you. You are their delight and their cause of every sacrifice. They intercede on your account for all the world, and their hidden lives are a profound witness to any who would allow their holiness to touch them. Yet they always profess only their poverty, lowliness, and guilt before you. They who are the boast of their Church and the glory of the ages, the masters of prayer and the exemplars of*

*discipline, groan because of their awareness of their failure to respond wholeheartedly to your word and to your grace.*

*They weep while they pray, sorry for their smallness and falsehood of heart, as compared to the greatness and truth of your own. Thank you for the sobering challenge they are to me. Thank you for the fundamental truth in which they live and which they are re-teaching me. For I can see that their sense of guilt is not a weakness of character in them, or a fearfulness of life. I rejoice to see that they are not craven or lacking in self-respect. Rather, they are always before you, and the impulse of their soul is that humility which expands love, gratitude, admiration, and zeal. They are alive more than I am because they are restless to be alive fully to you. Teach me, then, their littleness of spirit whereby they have become so great in love and so strong in your peace!*

The desert monk prays again:

"When I consider the multitude of my wicked works, re-membrances of that terrible judgment comes to my heart. Trembling takes hold of me, and I take refuge in Thee, O God, the lover of mankind. Turn not away Thy Face from me Who alone art without sin. Grant my wretched soul a godly fear before the consummation, and save me!"

# NOVEMBER
## A TIME TO VISIT ABRAHAM

### *Guest Master and Mentor*

NOVEMBER 4, TUESDAY

The monk appointed to be my informant in terms of my anthropological fieldwork is Abuna Sidrak. The name "Sidrak" is taken from the name of one of the three young men in the fiery furnace of the Book of Daniel: Shadrach, Meshach, and Abednego. Abuna Sidrak is a senior monk in this monastery and is the head guest master. He was appointed to the task of looking after me by the abbot, Anba Serabamon, because, among other things, having been well educated, he can speak English. It's expected that with my Arabic (being so poor), I will need someone to translate terms for me. He is a spiritual master now, by all accounts.

So Abuna Sidrak sees me from time to time to give me spiritual talks. Although this is not why I need to see him, it turns out that, since I am working on the cosmology of the Copts, including their cultural view of themselves and the role of their religion in their culture, listening to Abuna Sidrak's fervorinos and his reconstruction of the desert history of the monks is valuable to me, both for social science and for the very reasons that they have assumed I am here to begin with. Because, of course, how can I be here without my sojourn also being, on another and deeper level, a pilgrimage?

In pursuing my academic discipline, secular and even antithetical to religion as it is, it is becoming more and more evident that every facet of fieldwork in social science must, at the same time, admit to being a personal act of self-discovery. My own agendas are revealed in my investigations of Coptic culture and, for me as a monk, the revelation of self is a penitential work!

NOVEMBER 6, THURSDAY

> *Desert God,*
> *For days I have been smiling so broadly, I fear that I may look irreverent to these holy monks! You are purifying me from all my worldly preoccupations with painless delights. Every stone and ancient shard strewn across the sands pleases me. Every aspect of the monks, aged and novice, intrigues and blesses me. They are accustomed to this place of austere beauty. They are well worn into its pure submission to your hot sun, dry wind, cold nights, and endless horizons. Their faces, like the stones themselves, are baked and set into their desert niches. Yet they are alive, the stones and the faces, alive with obedience to your ways and the acceptance of your will.*
>
> *How I enjoy hearing the monks praise you through the night! Their chant is steady and sure; the clouds of smoke are thick with incense as they permeate the air, our skin, our clothes, and our souls. They are the prayer of the desert itself. The aspirations of every citizen of earth rise up through them to heaven. The monks praise you from the desert floor of the human heart. As you have said, if they would not, the rocks and stones themselves would start to sing (Luke 19:40)!*

## Gifts of Grapes

NOVEMBER 8, SATURDAY

A number of years ago, I read an account of a story in the hagiography of the early Desert Fathers that I have now actually experienced myself!

A few weeks ago, some pilgrims brought to the abbot a bowl of succulent grapes from the Nile Valley. Anba Serabamon thanked the guests very much and, when they left, he promptly presented the grapes to me as his visiting monk.

After I thanked the abbot, he left, and I decided to give the grapes to Abuna Sidrak, the guest master of the monastery who had been taking such good care of me. It was an act of gratitude on my part, and also a little calculus, that if I were to give him a gift, he might be even more forthcoming as a guest master in the future.

The guest master, it turns out, gave the grapes to his spiritual director and confessor in admiration for all of the virtues he had shown him. His spiritual director gave the grapes to the eldest monk in the monastery as a token of reverence and respect for his age. Being the resident anthropologist and conducting constant interviews, I learned that the eldest monk had promptly given the grapes to the youngest monk, since he had so recently left his home to come here. And so it went: the grapes slowly made their rounds in the monastery.

When I opened the door of my cell this morning, I found a gift from an anonymous donor, a bowl of raisins, in the doorway! So I wonder if those raisins were, in fact, the grapes that had recently made their rounds here. If they were, then probably everyone in the monastery benefited momentarily from them. Everyone, as it were, enjoyed that feast, though no one actually ate those grapes. However, I ate all the raisins myself!

### An Ancient Solitary

NOVEMBER 11, TUESDAY

Today when he came to see me, Abuna Sidrak told me that he was going to take me to the cell of the hermit, Abuna Elia. I'm looking forward to seeing him again, as our brief meeting in September highlighted my own entry into this monastery.

More than thirty years ago, Abuna Elia was part of the original group of disciples of the great monastic reformer, Abuna Mina el Muttawahad, who was later to become the Coptic Patriarch, Pope Kyrillos VI. To a large degree, Pope Kyrillos was responsible for the rejuvenation of monasticism in Egypt. He has long since died, of course, but in the 1940s and 1950s, almost single-handedly, he restored monastery after monastery, so great was the enthusiasm around him as a charismatic monastic reformer.

Abuna Mina el Muttawahad was called "the Solitary," although he was in and out of solitude as many of the Coptic solitaries have been in the past. He would live in the caves or out in the desert; then he would stride into the villages or into the cities, gather up disciples, inspire congregations, and head right back out into the desert again. This kind of commute has apparently been the rhythm of the Coptic monk and the desert holy man for hundreds of years. Pope Kyrillos conformed to this ancient pattern.

Anyway, in the 1940s and 1950s, he led a number of disciples out into the desert, some of whom have become rather famous in the Coptic Church. Abuna Matta el Meskeen, Matthew the Poor, who is now the Abbot of St. Macarius and one of the most famous, perhaps *the* most famous Coptic religious figure internationally, was one of those original disciples. Pope Shenouda III, while just a graduate student, years before he became bishop, was also one of the original disciples of Abuna Mina el Muttawahad. There were others as well: Abuna Samuel, later Anba (Bishop) Samuel, was a famous spokesman for the Coptic Church in ecumenical affairs. He was killed when he was seated next to Anwar Sadat at the time of Sadat's assassination. Anba Samuel was representing the Coptic Church in the parade that day when the gunmen got out of the truck and shot down everyone sitting on the presidential dais.

Abuna Elia was also one of the original company of Abuna Mina's followers. He is not publicly great; he is the only one who did not become a bishop or an abbot or a pope. But as much as he could, so long as he was able, he lived in the desert. He is now old and unfamous and, until recently, managed to remain in his original estate as a solitary.

Several years ago he was recalled out of the distant desert solitude, back to the environs of the Wadi Natroun. As noted earlier, he has now been called out of the solitude of the hills and the caves nearby to live entirely inside the walls of the monastery because of his advanced age and infirmity. So Abuna Elia groans now, I gather, because he is so besieged with all the sights and sounds of the monastery, most especially the pilgrims.

I'm looking forward, then, to being brought to his cell to meet him again, although I dread to further tax him. Like everyone else, I suppose he has also taken me to be a pilgrim. But, since I wear a habit, he must imagine me to be a pilgrim of a somewhat different nature.

### Renewed Acquaintance

NOVEMBER 13, THURSDAY

After the Kodes today, Abuna Sidrak reminded me that Abuna Elia was looking forward to seeing me. This is a big honor, Abuna Sidrak told me, and he assured me that this would be a great bless-

*Abuna Elia*

ing for me. At the same time, I could tell that he was a little bit apprehensive about the meaning of this meeting. Abuna Elia does not ask to see pilgrims. So far as I can tell, he has not asked to see *anyone* since he has come back to the monastery. Therefore, Abuna Sidrak is perhaps nonplussed that he has asked to see me when we had scarcely spoken before.

While I was waiting in the church after the Kodes, Abuna Sidrak came to tell me that it was time to meet Abuna Elia. We walked through the courtyard of the monastery, down a garden path, and into a region which is designated by signs, both in English and in Arabic, as strictly cloister. We passed a row of doors leading into adobe cells and finally came to the cell of Abuna Elia. He was seated in the doorway, waiting for us. He looked remarkable. His beard is one of the longest, whitest beards I have ever seen on a monk in Egypt. He looks like the stereotypical mountain guru. He has the whitest skin that I have ever seen on an Egyptian, bleached-looking. I'm told that this is from his many years of living out of sunlight, out of all light, while he dwelt in a cave, and that this and his ascetical diet have altered his complexion. He even has the palest eyes; he almost looks albino.

He greeted me with a very warm smile and the gentlest demeanor. At his feet was a cat which hovered by him, yet he never seemed to attend to it, or even to notice it. Abuna Elia had me be seated outside his cell where there was a stool for me and a chair for him. Abuna Sidrak introduced us and took his leave. The old monk spoke to me for a while, asking me what I am doing in the monastery, what my training has been in Scripture, and what I think about the monastic desert way of life and holiness.

He told me that the Egyptian monks in the monastery today *feel* everything which is appropriate to the monastic life, that is to say, they "affectively" (he didn't use the word) animate the monastic life as they should. Nevertheless, he said, their *understanding* of what they are doing is not as strong as their *feeling* for it. Their level of comprehension and intellection about the monastic life is somehow limited due to the scarcity of literature on the subject in Arabic. And if they understand less, he said, they tend to be somewhat inarticulate about the theological aspects of desert monasticism with anyone who asks direct questions about it. Indeed, this can be a virtue, because silence, brevity of words, is a sign of interior quietude.

But in their case, he assured me, it's not just a virtue; it's also a burden, and even more so for him because discourse along these lines is what Abuna Elia craves. They are not trained, he said, to be intellectual exponents of the monastic life or of the way of holiness. And how could they be? he sighed. Can the Copts re-open the School of Alexandria? No, their school is the Way of the Cross, and while that is the greatest of graces, it is also a way of inconsolable silences.

He finds this to be a solitude within a solitude, saying that even when he is in the company of his brother monks, as he has lately come to be, he is still very much alone. But in this case, his aloneness is tinged with a kind of regret, because when he was truly alone, without human company, that aloneness was sweetened by a sense of the divine presence. There is a certain sense of the absence of God when one is in company wherein he cannot freely talk about God, when he cannot fully share the mysteries he is enjoying about God.

### The New Isaac

So Abuna Elia has determined, and I don't know from what evidence, that he can speak to me about God in the manner he longs for. He was, I guess, very pleased to hear that I was trained in a seminary and had some years of Scripture. He was also pleased that I knew at least some Greek and even some Hebrew theological terms. As it turns out, Abuna Elia learned Greek and Hebrew during his many—at least ten—years of almost absolute solitude in the caves of the outer desert. During that time, he studied these two languages for the purpose of reading the Fathers of the Church and the Scriptures. He is thrilled that I am able to understand some of his terminology and that I'm taking notes on what he says. These two things he has yearned for since he has come back to the monastery.

He said to me finally, in a rather poignant way, that I shall be his "Isaac." When I asked him what he meant, he replied that Isaac was the son of Abraham in his old age, and that Abraham became fruitful when it was long past the time for him to be so. In this case, Abuna Elia believes that I am going to make him fruitful by hearing what he has to say, and by preserving the cumulative wealth of all of his reflections during his many years of solitude in the desert. I certainly do not think that I can make him fully fruitful for all those years. But I am glad to be able to interview him, to listen to his spiritual insights, and to record them for whatever purposes I may later apply them.

Finally, he told me that he will summon me at the times that he desires and that I should simply wait. I gather from this comment that I am not to ask to see him, but to wait until he calls me. This is perfectly congenial to me, inasmuch as my time (aside from the Psalmody) is otherwise mostly unstructured.

## Our Father in Faith

NOVEMBER 14, FRIDAY

Between Lauds and the Kodes, while it was still dark, Abuna Sidrak informed me while I was praying on the floor of the church that Abuna Elia will see me again this morning. After the Kodes he walked me through the inner cloister to the cell of Abuna Elia. It is peaceful, it is quiet at this time, so I imagine that, more often than not, when I am summoned to see Abuna Elia, it will be in the early morning.

Today Abuna Elia walked out to greet me. It was still too early for the pilgrims to come, but the kitchen had begun to make some tea and scones for them when they arrive. He called out to one of the *fellah*, the boys who work for the monastery, to bring us tea. Then he went to the kitchen and waited there to get some bread as well. Abuna Elia carried the bread over while the boy brought the tea. We talked, I sitting on the stool and he on his chair. His health seems improved since our first meeting.

He talked about, of all things, Abraham. He assured me that Abraham is indeed our father in faith—the father not only of the Jews and the Christians and the Moslems but also of the monk, the father of desert holiness, for Abraham was asked to sojourn in the desert for many years after he was called by God. In following God into the desert, he learned the way of prayer, the way of trust and obedience, and he could not help but also learn the way of solitude. Abuna Elia reminded me that, although Abraham had had a wife for all those years, his wife died and left him almost forty more years of life before he died himself. Indeed, not only was he alone

after the death of Sarah, but for some years before her death he became a solitary in the desert, so that, when she died, he had to
hurry back to her abode to perform the customary rites of grieving,
mourning, and burial.

Why was he separated from her? Abuna Elia pointed out that
the binding of Isaac, the *akidah*, had such a gravity, and cost him so
dearly, that, thereafter, all of his bonds became completely subordi-
nate to the knowledge of God and obedience to God. He became,
as it were, almost estranged from all things human. Abraham is
never recorded to have spoken a word to Isaac after the *akidah*, nor,
apparently, did he live with Sarah after this experience. His life had
been radically changed. And yet his detachment from this world, at
the same time, renewed him in his humanity, made him more fully
the "man" created in God's image, and made him capable of tran-
scending creatures by loving them.

Since the *akidah* was the origin of Abraham's spirituality, that is
to say, its deepest foundation, and since it made him the father of
Israel in fact, God blessed Abraham. He gave him back his son.
Isaac was now the medium of a "gift exchange," not just the recipi-
ent of a single passing favor.

From the point of view of Abuna Elia, this obedience on the part
of Abraham was a prefiguring of the Incarnation which took place at
the Annunciation. He said that because Mary surrendered herself
wholly and entirely to God's will in a manner most unique, God's
blessing, the blessing of the Incarnation, took place. God's presence
alighted in the world and all peoples have been blessed thereafter.
Indeed, Abuna Elia said that the *"Fiat"* of the Virgin Mary was, in
fact, what Abraham's obedience in some larger scheme of things
was designed to prefigure and to proclaim. Jesus is the Beloved Son
who becomes our "gift exchange" with the Father.

### A Frustrated Anthropologist

November 15, Saturday

I paced out the monastery, its walls, its buildings, its gardens,
and its paths so that I could scale a map. All eyes observed me writing my notes; nobody seemed pleased! And they were obviously
displeased by the appearance of my camera which, therefore, disappeared into the folds of my habit.

## "Here I Am"

NOVEMBER 16, SUNDAY

After the Kodes, I was summoned again to the cell of Abuna Elia. I was able to walk there myself this time, as I knew my way. My stool was already set up, and there was a little table arranged with more tea. Abuna Elia remembered how much sugar I take from my last visit. How gracious! He must be in his seventies. I had not expected him to be so careful about such details.

We returned to the story of Abraham and the unconditional submission of his will to God's when he replied "Here I am" to God's call (Genesis 22:1).

Abuna Elia said that the expression, "Here I am," is indicative of Abraham's complete openness and willingness to do as God requests. This willingness, this openness, is itself the foundation of the Covenant that God made with Israel and, indeed, the eternal Covenant that God made through Abraham with all peoples. God is asking us for an openness which is resonant with the openness of Abraham so that we can echo his words with greater and greater degrees of sincerity and intensity by also saying, "Here I am."

## The Mount of Moriah

In both the 12th and the 22d chapters of Genesis, God is showing Abraham a land: the land of Moriah. Abuna Elia reminded me that Moriah is identified in the Book of Chronicles as the very hilltop of Mount Zion, the place which will later become Jerusalem and the site of the future temple. It is upon Mount Zion, upon the hilltop of Moriah, in Solomon's Temple, that all of the sacrifices of a thousand years of temple life will take place. And Jesus' sacrifice on the Cross will likewise take place there. So it is, of course, a hillock of great sacrificial significance.

Perhaps it was a sacred place even before Abraham discovered it. Perhaps Melchizedek, already well known to Abraham for his priestly services, was offering sacrifices there. We are told that Melchizedek was the priest-king of Salem, and that Salem is to be identified with Jerusalem. Perhaps that is why Abraham recognized it when God showed him the mount on the horizon to which he was to take his son. All the world, Jew or Greek, godless or godly, seeks a place to engage God. On Mount Moriah, God provided one.

"In all of this," Abuna Elia said, "the desert was a teacher for Abraham. The desert teaches us how helpless we are, how much we depend upon one another for survival. It is with a complete sense of dependence, a complete sense of helplessness that we must approach God, and that we must approach one another in terms of possessiveness or control.

"Our relationships in the monastery," said Abuna Elia, "are filled with ambivalence. By complete openness and availability to one another, we are obedient to each other in matters of charity. We are at each other's service." He reminded me of St. Paul, who said, *"Humbly think of others as better than yourselves"* (cf. Philippians 2:3). "But at the same time," Abuna Elia added, "our relationships must be ordered by a surrender, a letting go, a sacrifice. We own no one; we possess no one. The chaste life is like this in general; the celibate life must be like this in particular, and the monastic life most especially so."

Abuna Elia assured me that the sacrifices we make in our lives as monks, as Christians, will always be enfolded in layer upon layer of the sacrifices that went before us. Ultimately, they will be enfolded in the sacrifice of Christ and his Cross on the Mount of Moriah. Our sacrifices do not achieve or attain merit or value in themselves—frequently because we do *not* agree to make them with the same undivided heart that Abraham did, or that Mary or Jesus did. But to whatever extent we may agree, that agreement is perfected when our sacrifices are enfolded in those holy sacrifices which were offered before us. We must always see our lives as gifts of offerings and sacrifices, as part of a larger movement of generosity from and to God: the gift exchange!

Abuna Elia reminded me that throughout his life, Abraham was asked to make sacrifices of separation. He had to leave his kinsfolk and his father's house and go out into the desert. Later he had to be separated from his nephew Lot. After that he had to be separated from his son Ishmael. Then there is this terrible story about the sacrifice that he was asked to make of Isaac. And finally, his wife predeceased him and we are told about the terrible separation he had to make at this time in his life. "All of these separations remind us of the cost of discipleship," said Abuna Elia. "They remind us of the abandonment about which Jesus protested on the Cross.

He felt that he had been forsaken by the rejection of Israel and by the desertion of his disciples and his friends. For him, all of these things became emblematic of the sense of the forsakenness of God. And yet Jesus remained faithful."

Abuna Elia said, "When God asks us to make heroic sacrifices, it is not because he is heedless of what we are giving up; he is profoundly aware of it. When we are offering gifts to God, we are not really offering much, unless, at the same time, we are also submitting all those things that are valuable to us. We must submit to God's will everything which is dearest to us, that which is our only one of something, that which we love, that which is even beyond our ordinary capacity to imagine losing. Otherwise, all of our prayers and protestations of fidelity are somewhat strategic and not genuine or sincere."

NOVEMBER 18, TUESDAY

*Tender Father,*

*"When Israel was a child," the prophet spoke in your name: "I loved him. Out of Egypt I have called my son" (Hosea 11:1). You, O God, summoned your "son" Israel through the desert in order, at last, to call him out of it. But why did you send your children into the desert to begin with? Was it that the desert was like the distance between us and you? Did we have to face the immensity of the chasm in order to turn back to the paradise of your friendship? Was the desert the realm we inherited when we disinherited your Covenant?*

*In that case, O God, you favored us to summon Israel back along the wilderness road. You favored your "son" to raise him up from the distractions of cities and towns, commerce and drudgery, to direct his way home to you. You taught him by this summons the magnitude of his hopelessness, unless you yourself would enter the desert too, from the other side, and close the distance by your own passage. You said to Moses, "I have come down to rescue them from the hands of the Egyptians, and lead them out of that land" (cf. Exodus 3:8). And to the prophet you said, "Out of Egypt I have called my son."*

*Indeed, St. Matthew records the prophet's poetic words and applies them with new poetry to Jesus—not just because as a child* *he sojourned in Egypt in the flight from Herod—but because he came **through** our desert to find us. He came **out** of our desert when at last he returned home to you, when he ascended from the "desert" of our suffering world and carried us to your divine embrace in the bosom of his humanity.*

*Mary and Joseph were the parents who carried Jesus from Egypt to Israel as a child. Mary of Magdala and Joseph of Arimathea sent your Son back to you from our desert when they lovingly buried him after his crucifixion. The author of the biblical text discerns the wonderful pattern of your Providence in these themes.*

*I thank you for the pattern of your Providence in my life. I thank you for the emissaries of your Son who have entered my desert exile and summoned me back to you. I thank you for the desert now all about me. Here my heart turns toward remembering this grace you have given me by helping me forget the distractions I have contrived till now to evade you.*

*Your Providence has sent me a loving family and firm friendships. Through them, you raise me up and give me courage to face the obstacles in my own character and the troubles of my generation. With them, I am strengthened to journey on through the desert which leads back to you. Remind me, Tender Father, that when you send loneliness, emptiness, and humiliation, you love me best of all by drawing me farther along the desert road toward the Promised Land of union with you.*

## Monastic Differences

NOVEMBER 20, THURSDAY

I came to the library today and was looking through some Coptic manuscripts relating to their history and the organization of the monastery when Abuna Tadros, the librarian, saw me and asked me to sit with him by his desk to speak for a while.

The usual tea was brought and we began to discuss both the monastery here in the desert and my monastery back in the States. Abuna Tadros asked me about its organization, its works, its temperament, its spirituality, its kinds of prayers and missions. Actually, I've been somewhat dreading these questions, since the monasteries in Egypt strike me as being so much more devout.

The monasteries in the States, by contrast, might seem lax, and I did not wish to be the bearer of that kind of disappointing news.

He saw that I was hesitant to answer, so he asked me specific questions. "Does each of the monks in your monastery own a car?" he asked me.

"No," I answered, "certainly not. It would be impossible for every monk to own a car. It would be unacceptable."

"Really?" he said. "I would have expected that every American has a car whether he is a monk or not, and that no American would settle for any kind of life in which he did not possess at least one car."

I thought about his remark, and I replied that it would still be inconsistent with the monastic life. Then he said, "You are great monks in the United States if you can resist the pull of your culture to that extent."

He asked me other questions. "Does every monk have his own personal bank account and his own personal income?"

"No," I said. "Our incomes are absorbed by the monastery; we have no personal wages." He found this remarkable as well, inasmuch as Americans are bound to be interested in their annual income, in their wage and tax bracket. So he was surprised that we could also transcend our culture to that degree.

I know that in the Western Church monks often compare one monastery unfavorably to another, especially to their own, on some level of analysis. But here, Abuna Tadros seemed to be so secure in who he is and what his monastery is that he did not need to make disadvantageous comparisons.

I went on to describe to Abuna Tadros the most significant difference which I noticed between our monasteries. "Our Western monastery is a collective reality under an abbot. Its greatest emphasis is on communal life and on fraternal love, a communal way of worshiping God through liturgical rites. Whereas," I said, "it is my opinion that this Coptic monastery emphasizes individual perfection and holiness, the virtue of monastic life which is cultivated interiorly. It seems that the primary relationship here is that between each monk and his spiritual father." While Abuna Tadros agreed with me that this is a significant difference, as our conversation progressed, he noted that we American monks are not nearly so communal as I had indicated, and that we allow a great deal of individual variation. That which I had been concerned about as a kind of laxity, he interpreted as "idiorhythmia": the conformity of the monastic ideal to a particular monk in his prayer life and in his relationship to a spiritual father.

What Abuna Tadros heard me say was not so much that individually we are lax, but that there is a great deal of latitude for each monk to determine, responsibly, the trajectory of his religious life. Perhaps Abuna Tadros was being generous in his assessment. Surely he was, but it's also true that so much of what the Western Church has achieved in recent years in terms of the evolution of religious life has been in the direction of personal accountability and responsibility. I don't know that it has always worked out as it was intended, but I'm sure that Abuna Tadros is right. If each monk had cultivated a spiritual direction, a spiritual-father relationship, then so much of what was envisioned by these adaptations in religious life in the last several decades since the Second Vatican Council would have come to pass.

### Coptic Prayer

November 21, Friday

Lauds this morning began as usual at 3:00 A.M. and lasted until 6:00 A.M. I should probably note by now my cumulative impressions of the Coptic morning prayer. I guess the most outstanding thing about it is that my legs ache. Most of it is done while standing! Something like seventy-five psalms are chanted in the same way we do in the Western Church: in choirs, antiphonally, back and forth. The monks have no chairs, however; they don't even have places to lean against. They simply stand in the body of the church. So, after thirty-five or forty-five minutes, there is an ache in the legs.

The monks use incense constantly during the chanting of the psalms. The smoke is so dense that one can sometimes barely breathe. After a while, with legs aching and the air filled with smoke, one feels that he is being gently swayed back and forth to the droning rhythm of their chant. It is a quarter-tone chant, that very Arabic-sounding music which is so trying to Western ears. But, little by little, I have become adjusted to it, and it seems to me almost hypnotic.

I am overwhelmed sometimes by the feel, by the mood of the choir. The sense to which I find it most comparable is, oddly, that of being swung back and forth by my grandfather when I was a child. It was what he loved to do with us, and what we loved to have done. And no matter how often he did it, we always said to him, "Swing me again." There was no end to our interest, our delight, in this motion.

Swaying back and forth with the psalms and the smoke and the aches and the pains is something which, while tiring on the one hand, is oddly refreshing and delightful on the other. Perhaps this is the nature of liturgical music and liturgical prayer. Of course, so much more could be added to make it interesting. If it were a theatrical production, constant novelty could be introduced, the kind of creativity which surprises people from moment to moment. But novelty is not what this kind of liturgical rite requires. It needs a certain sameness, a sense of something being received, something so "at home" with oneself that one can imagine doing it hours and hours on end, days proceeding upon days without number.

Perhaps "hypnotic" is the wrong word for what one experiences in this liturgical rite. It is the liturgy itself which cannot be reduced to something else. It has its own mode of interest, its own form of engagement of the soul. One does not try to muster up in himself a sense of God nor a sense of Christ. The monastic and liturgical rites presume that God is present, that the risen Christ is there in the midst of the praying community. This is understood so completely that what might otherwise seem to the outsider to be unrelentingly dull is, for the monk, something quite engaging and life-giving. It is something that summons him, even challenges him, to fuller participation in the mysteries of God. There is in it, then, a whole range of paradoxes: it is both comforting and challenging. The monk feels at home, and yet he feels summoned forward. He feels that he is in the midst of something utterly familiar, and yet also he feels that he is in the midst of something completely otherworldly, something altogether new and unheard of.

The monks reminded me from time to time, in settings other than the liturgy, that unless one's soul is somehow right with God—at least in terms of penance and the monastic Office—the choir and the liturgical rites of the monastery will seem to be pure, continual penance. One must escape from them in that case. I recall how American Christians, and sometimes even monks, are constantly referring to their watches during worship—and I sigh.

## *Arabic Lessons*

NOVEMBER 23, SUNDAY

This afternoon after lunch, I had my first lesson in Arabic, that is, my first lesson in Egypt. It was with an employee of the monastery, a young man from one of the villages. His name is Hanee. Hanee needs to learn English, he says, and I need to learn Arabic—or at least learn more than what I had already learned at the university. Abuna Sidrak thinks that, at least for a while, this might be a happy combination. So I began my lessons. Hanee thinks that the best way to learn Arabic is through studying the texts associated with the Scriptures. Since, as he quite rightly reasons, I already know the Scriptures in English, I shall be able to understand them in Arabic because they are familiar to me. So we began working on Scripture texts today.

Hanee wants to learn English because, he said, "English is the avenue to all things shiny and new." He already speaks Arabic, of course, and Coptic—at least enough Coptic to participate in the prayer life of the Church. He said (in Arabic) that "the Coptic language is the road, the *tarek*, the avenue, to all things ancient and true."

The manner by which the employees of the monastery pray when they come to the Kodes or to the monks' prayers is very touching. They regard their monks with great reverence, with a deep respect. This is remarkable inasmuch as they work with the monks in the fields, in various crafts and works of the monastery every day, for weeks and months on end. It is a testament to the goodness of both the employees and their monks that such a deep respect continues to abide when they labor together over a long period of time. The monks teach the employees to perfect their Coptic language skills so they can better participate in the prayers of the monastery.

Most of the employees of the monastery are very young. To see them studying and memorizing their Coptic prayers reminds me of my earliest memories in the Roman Church, when the language of preference was still Latin. These unlettered villagers pray in a language they do not understand, by and large, and yet it seems to nourish them completely.

There are Coptic people who object, just as Catholics objected, to praying in a language which they do not understand. But the Coptic monks are insisting, and so apparently is the hierarchy of this Church, that understanding the words of a prayer is the least important part of the meaning and the value of the prayer. The monks remind me that *"the Spirit intercedes for us with groans too deep for words"* (cf. Romans 8:26) and, therefore, when you are groaning, when you are aching, when you are too tired to participate intellectually in the psalmody, you are still praying. The Holy Spirit is unlocking the depths of that which lies within. Sometimes when the mind is fully engaged and thinking in its own terms and categories, it will not release the inward soul to discourse with God. Sometimes the mind must work itself through its desire to control and come to a kind of humility, a relaxation of its powers, so that the Spirit might work at deeper currents than those which the mind employs.

So I think of the words of the psalmist: *"Like a weaned child on its mother's lap, so is my soul within me"* (Psalm 131:2). Just as the weaned child doesn't speak, and yet communes with its mother so completely, we commune with our Mother Church. Our hearts are united in prayer before God, not so much by our faculties of understanding and the employment of our intellects as by the submission of our affects, our thirsts, and our appetites to our trust in God, and to a good order among each other in charity.

My language exchange with Hanee had to proceed, first of all, through a gift exchange. I understand now that no meaningful contacts can be established in Coptic society without the giving and receiving of gifts. So I gave him rosary beads, and he gave me a little prayer book, one that could easily fit in a vest pocket. It was a book of Arabic and Coptic prayers. Judging from its worn pages, I realized that this must have been Hanee's prayer book for many, many years. But he was delighted to give it to me. I said I could hardly accept from him something so personal as his own daily prayer book. He responded by saying that his prayers would be sanctified if a monk would take the book he used for prayer and use it himself. Surely, he said, I would remember to pray for him when I look at the pages and consider that they had been worn by his efforts to pray. He considers his prayers to have been failures until and unless they are gathered into someone else's prayers which are succeeding.

Of course, it is not true that his prayers are a failure, or that my prayers are more successful. But what he said in his own simple way reminds me that all of our prayers are failures unless they are conjoined to the prayers of the One who does know how to pray. That is the work of the Spirit: to gather our prayers into the prayer of the One who knows how to offer the true sacrifice of praise and obedience: Christ Jesus. Christ Jesus in the Garden; Christ Jesus on the Cross; Christ Jesus in the Upper Room with his disciples after the Resurrection; Christ Jesus at the right hand of the Father, Christ Jesus who intercedes and prays for us, and with us, day and night before his heavenly Father.

## The Ark in the Desert

NOVEMBER 24, MONDAY

After the Kodes in the monastery church, I celebrate my own Mass privately. It is later in the morning by then, and I often take a walk. Like some of the monks here, I try to avoid the press of the pilgrims who come on the weekends.

Today, I walked out to the monastery Deir el Suriani, or the Monastery of the Syrians, named after the Syrian monk who established it centuries ago. Many monks from a variety of national and ethnic backgrounds came to Egypt after the fourth century to establish monasteries and to share in the special genius of monasticism that had been initiated in the Egyptian desert.

I walked around the perimeter of the monastery and counted my paces. It's an oddly shaped monastery, unlike any of the others I've visited so far. It is twenty paces or so in width, and one hundred and twenty paces in length. The whole complex gives the impression of being an oblong box with steep walls rising up from the desert floor. It is a completely self-contained box in which the life of the monastery abides.

When I came back to the monastery of Deir St. Bishoi, I asked Abuna Arsenious why Deir el Suriani is so oddly shaped. Abuna Arsenious answered that it has the general proportions of the Ark of Noah as described in the sixth chapter of the Book of Genesis. So I looked it up. Sure enough, the Ark of Noah was three hundred cubits long and fifty cubits wide, so both the Ark of Noah and the Monastery of el Suriani are built on a ratio of six to one. I guess

*The façade of Deir el Suriani.*

the Ark of Noah looked like a large oblong box too. Of course, this intentional duplication of the same ratio is an indication that the monks of Deir el Suriani, like the ancient Desert Fathers in general, saw their monastery in the very same way that they regarded the Ark of Noah at the time of the great flood. It was a place of refuge, a place in which something of God's original good creation was preserved from destruction in the harsh environment of the world outside, almost a kind of original innocence. An original, created good is also protected inside the monastery.

In what sense do the monks see themselves in a place of refuge like the Ark of Noah? In a variety of ways, actually. They have come from the world outside, just as the animals came two by two into the Ark, so they know very well what is out there. It is not that they are looking down from an ivory tower in a denigrating way at the world outside. They have been members of both the monastic and the secular communities, so they can speak authoritatively about what they know. They know that, for them, remaining in the world after they had felt or heard the call from God to enter the monastery could have been the cause of their dissolution. They would have been swept up in the tides of secularity and corruption. Secularity might not pull down those who are called by God to live out in the world, but for those who are called to a different kind of life there may not be sufficient grace in the rejection of their God-given vocation to remain in the world safely. So they see themselves as somehow saved from the dangerous vicissitudes of secular life.

But there are other associations that the monks make with Noah and his Ark. They imagine that in living inside the monastery there is a dignity of faith that is shared among the members. It is a dignity that preserves them from the faithlessness—the doubt—that is a flood everywhere else in the world, one which can pull the unsuspecting soul down into its undertow. Likewise, the world is filled with storms and troubles, occasions of anxiety and anguish. In the monastery, by comparison, the monks see themselves living a life of holy leisure where the rhythm of life is established for prayer, where God is central.

But the analogy goes even deeper than that. The monastery is a still, quiet place, just as the inside of the Ark must have seemed quiet compared to the raging storms outside. A still, quiet place is a place appropriate to the prayer of the heart as well as the prayer of the community. Life in the monastery is a life of charity; life in the world outside is a life of desperation, just as it was in the time of Noah. Outside the Ark, every living thing was in dire straits, scratching, clawing, trying to survive. Inside the walls of the Ark, God preserved the peaceable kingdom. There the lion lay down with the lamb.

After the Ark landed on the Mount of Ararat and its inhabitants redispersed over the world, it must have remained for some time as a shrine of Divine Providence and human obedience. According to the flood story in Genesis, the rainbow was given as a sign, and the Monastery of el Suriani remains as a witness to that Providence.

## Tradition

NOVEMBER 25, TUESDAY

Within the grounds of Deir el Suriani, there is a great tamarind tree, a huge tree with a trunk so large that many people arm-to-arm can hardly encircle it. It's a remarkable sight, because scarcely a shrub or a blade of grass grows in the desert in this area, and to see this tree fabulously large and luxuriant is almost miraculous. In fact, that's exactly what the monks say of it: that long ago when St. Ephraim, the founder of the monastery, arrived in the place, he planted his staff there just before he died. According to legend, his staff sprouted leaves and sent out roots and became a living tree. So now, many centuries later, that tender shoot of a tree has become this great tamarind.

In my mind, as a true Westerner, I tried to imagine a plausible, natural sequence of events whereby such a tree might grow in the middle of the Sahara. I thought about a seed which might have been dropped by a bird during one of those very rare desert rainstorms. If the seed fell in a place that was relatively low-lying, perhaps even into a muddy crevasse, its small roots, which would have sprouted in the moisture, might have been able to recede deeper and deeper down into the sands of the desert. At length, the roots may have tapped into an underground reservoir that was somehow closer to the surface than usual. It might have happened that, given a steady supply of water, the plant continued to grow where nothing else had grown or would grow. It might have drawn its nourishment from the underground spring and eventually grown into this great tamarind. The Scriptures speak about a tree that draws its life-giving water from a spring and, therefore, its leaves never grow old and its fruit is always fresh (cf. Psalm 1:3).

While I might be inspired by this natural sequence of events whereby a miraculous tree grows in the desert, the tradition of the staff of the abbot who founded the monastery has deeply symbolic meaning. The monks are describing the value of drawing up from a secret recess of the past, a long-standing tradition: a great and wide and deep heritage around which the faithful can gather in high aspiration, in holiness of life and holy charity in the middle of the desert of this world. They gather around that great tree, like a center of their world, an axis around which the rhythm of their life revolves. I believe that this is really a better way to see and appreciate a tradition.

Tradition is not just a static thing, a dead standard against which we make comparisons. Like that tree, it is something living and organic. It is something around which we can find life and inspiration, something upon which we can look with wonder. We wonder at how those who went before us did what they did, and how we might be able to follow their example, under their inspiration. Ultimately, a miraculous tree like this is a sign of the Resurrection, a sign of the power of the Lord to be alive in our midst and to call us out of our aridity, out of our deadness, into a fully realized human life.

Abuna Arsenious told me that the staff of the founder abbot is like the staff of Aaron in the Book of Exodus. That staff bore fresh blossoms and leaves when Aaron planted it in the ground. Aaron did so because the people of Israel were faithless at that moment. He wished to give them a sign that God was alive and present in their midst, and that he was greater than all of their doubts and fears. If dead wood could come to life, then a people filled with death could also rise to new life.

It is perhaps in the same way that the Church continually celebrates the iconography of the Crucifix in so many ways, in so many art forms, in so many sculptures. Here, what seems to be dead wood is a life-giving tree planted in our midst. The power of the living Lord is shown forth upon it so that we might be invigorated, that we might be inspired and take heart.

The monastery is like the Ark of the Covenant made by Moses. The "staff of Aaron," the universal, holy priesthood of Christ, is planted therein in their common prayer. Life in the monastery revolves around the Eucharist, the Bread of Life, like the fall of manna in the desert. There is also a life of holy *lectio* in the monastery, a life of meditation on God's Word, the Living Word, the Word made flesh, analogous to the tablets of stone which were placed in the Ark by Moses. In all these respects, the monastery is rightly regarded by the monks as being like the Ark of Noah and the Ark of the Covenant.

NOVEMBER 26, WEDNESDAY

*O Sovereign Lord,*

*You are the Master of this world, although your mastery is hidden and your authority is ignored. You spoke occasionally of the owner of an estate who went away on a journey while the laborers forgot his rules or neglected his rights. Some fell asleep and were not ready to welcome him back. Some became abusive with the household. Some neglected to invest the resources given to them, and some refused to make payment back to him at the proper time. Always the absence of the lord is the background of their folly.*

*But you, O Lord, want our love to be the motive of our virtue. You wish us to love you freely and give our reverence sincerely. Your "absence" is only the space that our wills require to freely choose, that our hearts require to genuinely love. If you pressed more closely upon us, our bond to you would always be the reflex of our fear. But if you were farther away, we might forget about the opportunity for your friendship altogether. As it is, you are nearer than any other to me, yet so gently near that I could overlook you. You are infinitely far away and other from me, but I cannot evade the intuition of your existence.*

*This is the paradox of the "middle-distance" by which you created me and through which you call me to union. Your Holy Cross is the visible sign of your greatness reduced for the survey of our little vision. Yet, marvelously, the love you bear on it is in no way diminished from the Love you are and have agelessly shared within the Communion of Heaven.*

*This desert is my blessed retreat into the "middle-distance" of your Presence: arid and abundant; silent and singing; empty and filled; lonely and alluring; fearsome and friendly. Here I see the*

*Cross more brightly: fallen down and lifted up; dying and rising; humiliated and exalted; tragic and glorious; abandoned, yet affirmed forever.*

*Let me never forget you in any place I go. Let the grace of this place carve a niche in my soul. May the solitude of this Holy Wilderness become the center of my present memories and my future friendships. May I always love for the sake of the beloved and for the sake of love's Source, O Lord, and not for my own satisfaction.*

## Advent Vigils

NOVEMBER 29, SATURDAY

On every Saturday of Advent, the monks in the monastery keep an all-night vigil called *kyak*. It is a night during which many hymns are sung and many prayers are prayed. It is a night of constant meditation on the mysteries of Advent, of expectation, of yearning and longing for the fullness of the Lord's presence. It is most especially, then, a night in which the Virgin Mary is honored in the monastery. For as the monks sing of her during this night, she is the embodiment of all of human openness and human desire for the fullness of God's coming. She represents the fulfillment of the highest hope of this earth to attain union with God.

There are songs that compare her to the Ark of the Covenant in ways similar to the meditation about the monastery. Mary housed within her body, under her heart, the same three elements contained in the Ark made by Moses. The Ark held the staff of Aaron, the high priest; Mary carried in her womb the High Priest himself. As Aaron's staff, once dead wood, blossomed in the desert as a sign to inspire faith, so Christ rose from death as a sign of our eternal life. As the Ark of the Covenant contained the manna, so Mary bore in herself the "Bread of Life come down from heaven." As the first Ark contained stone tablets whereon God's word was inscribed, so Mary received and held within her womb the Word made flesh.

They sing about these things, the monks, with the many pilgrims who come here. One has only to see them to realize that, for them, these are not abstract theological ideas. They're not even just good poetry. For these people, even for the simplest of the laity who are poor villagers, who wear mere rags, these meditations on Mary are living truths. She is their Mother, their Mother in faith and in hope. She is the one who receives Christ and makes him available to them. In these truths they place great store and find great consolation.

As the night progresses, I see the large families of the poor who gather in the monastery church. They huddle together on their pillows right on the floor, little clusters of them, one lying against the other, warming one another, praying and sleeping. All these things are conjoined together in acts of creaturely piety, so sincere, so basic, so simple. I can almost imagine, for the first time, what the spirituality of the ancient world might have been like in old Bethlehem or in the hill country of Judea, as the people there longed for the salvation of God, for the revelation of the Good News. These Copts must share with all poor people of all ages a certain simplicity which Christ Jesus must regard as blessed: a quality which predisposes them to be totally receptive to his love and his grace.

# ✴ DECEMBER

## A TIME OF SIGNS: *CAELUM ET TERRA*

### *Desert Warfare*

#### DECEMBER 2, TUESDAY

I had a conference with Abuna Sidrak today. He told me about the desert monastic understanding of the Evil One, of Satan. He said that the monks commonly use the word *afarit* to denote the external, personal force of evil in the world, the fallen angelic race. He said that there is an engagement with the Evil One in the life of all Christians after baptism and that, rather paradoxically, the further one grows in holiness, the greater is the possibility of that combat, that spiritual warfare. He said that no one passes through this life exempt from the possibility of attack, the possibility of temptation and struggle. Just as Jacob wrestled with the angel whom God sent, we are always wrestling with the fallen angels. Abuna Sidrak said that it is something which is especially a problem with the monks; they are always struggling against evil in the desert.

Certainly, as a novice, I remember reading about the Desert Fathers, about their constant warfare and their fearsome struggles with temptations, direct and indirect, even their visitations from the Evil One in a variety of guises. The Fathers of the Church also spoke a great deal about this subject, and it is rather remarkable, by contrast, how little the struggle with evil is mentioned in contemporary circles of spirituality in the West. Hollywood is far more interested in this combat than are seminaries.

Abuna Sidrak reminded me that the mission of Jesus can be viewed from a variety of angles, including the perspective of exorcism and deliverance. This is certainly true. We can see the mission of Jesus as a work of liberation from ignorance, from oppression, from hunger. We can see it as a healing from disease, sickness, and woundedness. We can see it as the restoration of our original nature, and we can see it as a deliverance from evil, interior to us or around us. The miracle stories in the Gospels all revolve around these basic themes.

Abuna Sidrak said that all of these activities are aspects of the same single work. Jesus anticipated the efficacy of the Cross by a variety of dramatic acts throughout his public life, and he brought all of them to a climactic unity and completion in his sacrifice on the Cross.

The Fathers, Abuna Sidrak noted, were always comparing the individual story of a soul to the history of Israel. Moses grieved because the Hebrew people were longing to return to slavery. They groaned because of the heavy responsibilities that freedom gave them (they actually remembered, of all things, the better diet that they had in Egypt: the condiments, the spices and the herbs that they had been able to enjoy as slaves).

So the soul, liberated by grace, redeemed by the Cross of Jesus, is constantly engaged in reminiscences of what was possible before baptism. Even if it was an infant baptism, there are somehow regrets about what could have been, regrets about what was missed as a result of being associated with the Gospel from the beginning. We are always looking for the "condiments," and, Abuna Sidrak rightly pointed out, more and more throughout the world, because of the West's media, the "condiments" of the non-baptismal life are ever available to tempt us. The world, the flesh, and the devil: these three things form a kind of covert conspiracy—not so covert nowadays—to draw us into slavery again. I sigh when I consider how many Religious Sisters, Brothers, monks, and priests I have met in America who virtually disqualify the validity of their vows on the basis that they made them when they were too young to appreciate all the opportunities they were giving up!

Abuna Sidrak does not think that the life of grace is a life of slavery whereby we lose our freedom to enjoy pleasure. Rather, he thinks that the Evil One draws us into a life of slavery to pleasure—or at least to what we think are pleasures. And then, Abuna Sidrak said, there is not even much enjoyment in them. When we first sold ourselves to them, they appeared to be pleasures, but the more we attained them, the less joy they gave us, because it is not the intention of the Evil One to give human beings pleasure. And if he should tempt us to pleasure, he would do so only by giving us the minimum of it—even just the illusion of it. So the whole world will be filled one day with people appearing to be happy, appearing to enjoy all of their wealth and possessions. Yet so unhappy and miserable will they be, that they will not allow themselves to appear as they really are. They will lie about it and try to deceive others about how awful they really feel; otherwise they will feel absolutely alone.

This strikes me as a remarkably intuitive grasp of the way in which the world has gone, with the media fashioning for us the appropriate appearances whereby we should look happy with all that we have acquired. But, in fact, not only are we unhappy, we are unable to allow anyone to know it; we are unable to show how hollow all of this has become. This is the new mythology, the new dogma that must not be violated. TV commercials do nothing so much as serve up momentary vignettes of seemingly happy people, made so by the endless acquisition of whatever the market is promoting. I come from a culture where even people of faith long to be enslaved by the markets and the media, not unlike the Hebrews who longed to return to slavery while on their exodus journey.

Abuna Sidrak said that the Evil One traditionally appeared to the monks in the desert under three forms: the beast, a woman, or an image suggesting some kind of phantom or ghost-like apparition. The beast, he said, was designed to instill fear; the woman was designed to tempt us with our own weaknesses. And, in the case of the phantom-like images, the Evil One's intention was to confuse us, to befuddle us, to make us unsure of what is real, what is true.

He also noted that the Evil One sometimes simply sends us evil people to harass us. Sometimes people carry with them intimations of evil, yet we mustn't necessarily blame them per se, since God has permitted it for us to be tested. He said that the Wadi Natroun has been called "the valley of devils" for a long time by the monks. Ah, that they should call their own home so! The devils in the valley of the Wadi Natroun no longer appear so much in images to confuse or tempt us. They sometimes appear in confreres, rather, who unwittingly act as agents to upset or anger or sadden us. This is the struggle now; it is really about whether or not we can endure and persevere and grow in our vocation.

Abuna Sidrak said that we are supposed to do battle with the Evil One by our humility before God. We must be alert to recognize temptations as early as possible and to nip them in the bud. By doing so, we can prevent the attractions from overpowering us for, he noted, they can quickly grow in us. They send out their roots rapidly, and soon we find that they preoccupy the majority of our thoughts in one form or another.

When the Christian monk prays the psalm verse *"Happy the man who shall smash your little ones on the rock"* (Psalm 137:9), he has this very complex situation of evil and temptation in mind. Babylon's power to enslave, and the devil's power to tempt, might first suggest themselves with little faults, but they will one day grow big enough to rule over us.

Abuna Sidrak said the Evil One improves on our desires; he makes things seemingly more sweet. But things are not more sweet. Life simply becomes more base. Our senses are lowered in terms of their capacity for true enjoyment. While we appear to be enjoying more and more, we are actually experiencing less and less pleasure. It is Jesus, he said, who came to give us life to the fullest; he raised our capacity for joy to the highest level possible.

In any place where we are, there will be fleshly desires, Abuna Sidrak added, desires that are interior and private. This gives the Evil One an occasion to tempt or to test us. But these occasions of temptation are by no means sins; they are, in fact, opportunities to grow in holiness. They are occasions to rise in nobility. But if we should fail, it is because we have lived internally in desperation and in fear.

The devil has convinced us that unless we grasp for what will satisfy us, it will not be given to us by God; that God is not so generous, apparently, as he claims to be. So we fear, in our own desperation, that we must place our priorities ahead of God's, and make our own anxieties and our own neediness greater than our trust in his solicitude or his Providence.

Abuna Sidrak said that the tongue is frequently the special foothold of temptation, either in terms of gluttony or in terms of malicious or deceptive speech. So the taming of the tongue—especially as St. James speaks about it in his letter (James 3:1-13)—is the primary ascetical work of the monk, and of every Christian. It is by fasting, most of all, that we are able to train the tongue. Fasting from all kinds of food, in all kinds of ways, deprives the tongue of the prior right it would like to claim over our body.

Abuna Sidrak said that fasting from words, fasting from a volume of speech, being willing to humbly accept the yoke of silence and quietude—this too deprives the tongue of the mastery of our hearts and minds. The tongue is a very useful tool for the art of love and for the art of prayer, but it is also the means by which we afflict others and even our own selves. So it must, more than anything else, be called into holy obedience to the Gospel. It must become the locus from which we allow the grace of the Gospel and the merit of the Cross to win for us a liberation from evil.

I find very much of what Abuna Sidrak said to be congenial, consistent with both what has been revealed in the spiritual classics and with what is apparent in human nature. I wonder, always, why so little is said about the province of evil in the modern world and in the modern Church. It strikes me that in earlier times no one doubted the realms of good and evil: the one God and his omnipotent power versus the darker realm of disobedience filled with fallen angels. In those days, there were abundant signs of such realities. But in our day, when so many people, at least ostensibly, doubt both realities, then God in his heaven seems to give fewer signs. God wishes us to live a life of faith, not a life of entertainment fed by continual signs. As Jesus pointed out, *"A wicked generation demands signs"* (cf. Matthew 12:39).

The Evil One, likewise, for altogether different purposes, may hide his signs and obscure his art, for it is by far the most cunning aspect of evil that he should deceive us with regard to his purposes. Our not knowing what he intends or what he does leaves the soul open for a greater conquest on his part. And, indeed, confusion and lies, deceptions as to what is real or what is true have been his art from the beginning. So, if he can cause fear, as so many people experience nowadays; if he can cause all kinds of temptations of the flesh, as so many people suffer nowadays; if he can cause confusion as to his own existence, then he does what he has always done. He does it perhaps better now than ever, because of our inability to recognize his agency. This seems to be consistent with the contemporary experience of the Western Church.

### Blessings for Pilgrims

DECEMBER 4, THURSDAY

I've been observing pilgrims who come to the monastery. Rarely do the monks consider them to be sources of diabolic temptation, though surely they test the patience of the monks. But this is the test of compassion and charity. The pilgrims, for their part, see the monks as sources of divine blessing, sources of *barakah*. They seek from the monks God's grace, because they believe that the monks are the proximate source of blessing that he has established for them. They come out into the desert; they leave their homes, their places of business, of work, even their places of failure and sin and frustration so that they will be in a place available to holiness, not just geographically but, if there is such a thing, in the landscape of the soul. By being pilgrims, they are in a place that is open to a special channel of divine assistance.

How do the monks bless them? In ways that are established and conditioned by their history, even by their culture. If the pilgrims somehow manage to touch the hands of a monk, they believe that to be a blessing, especially if they can kiss his hand. If they manage to hold onto the ankle or the feet of a monk, they consider that to be a source of blessing. It is an even greater blessing if they can kiss the feet of the monk.

In all of these situations, the monk appears to try to pull away. He seems reluctant to allow his hands or his feet to be touched or to be kissed. But it's part of the give-and-take of the relationship between the monk and the pilgrim. It's almost a kind of choreography of reluctance and desire: reluctance on the monk's part, and desire on the part of the pilgrim. And yet both the reluctance of the monk and the desire of the pilgrim respect the intention of the other.

The pilgrims want the monk to place his hands upon their head, or they will place his hands upon their head if they can do so, or they will place his hands on the head of someone they want to be blessed. Their desire just to touch his hand reminds me so much of the story in the Gospel of the woman who touched the hem of the garment of Jesus.

Pilgrims who manage to elicit from the monk a small prayer obtain his blessing; even the merest words "God bless you" are sufficient. If they can obtain an object of the monk, especially an object associated with his prayer life, such as a prayer book or his hand-cross, or if they can kiss his hand-cross, they feel especially blessed. If they have an icon, a holy picture that they can touch to him, then touch to themselves, they obtain a blessing.

Pilgrims like to take the cross in the monk's hand and put it over their head; they like to touch their forehead to his hand-cross, or hold onto it for a time. They ask if they can have custody of it for an afternoon, or an evening, or overnight. They like to take it home for a while because someone at home is sick, and the person wants the blessing of the monk. If they buy a hand-cross themselves and ask the monk to hold it and then give it back to them, that can be a source of blessing.

If they can induce the monk to take a walk with them, no matter what the topic of their conversation, whether they like the monk or not, they are joyful to receive it as a blessing. If they can persuade the monk to eat a morsel of food they have brought, they feel they have been blessed. If they can obtain from him a glass of tea or a bit of food, they feel especially blessed. If they give the monk some food and he returns it to them, blessed, they feel they themselves have been blessed.

They like to get the monk's signature. They ask him to write his name in their Bible or their prayer book, or in a textbook. If he writes his name on a study sheet they are using to prepare for an exam, they feel they have a special blessing for taking that exam. To take a picture of a monk or, better yet, to have their own picture taken standing next to the monk is a blessing. Getting the promise of the monk's future prayers is regarded as a special kind of blessing.

If, when the monk happens to be out of the monastery, visiting the Patriarch in Cairo, visiting a church, giving a mission or giving talks, they can persuade him to come to their house and have dinner, they are blessed. Better yet, having a dinner that lasts so late that they can persuade the monk to stay in their house overnight, is the *greatest* blessing that anyone could hope for. The house is blessed, the family is blessed, everything they own is blessed; even their future is blessed.

Of course, one can view all this as primitive and superstitious, or one can see it as a desire for God welling up from the deepest part of the human soul. Where do we best intuit the presence of

God but in the primal desire to be hospitable to others, to give generously, to prevail upon others in charity, to pour ourselves out from our hearts in acts and gestures of love? So I do not regard this behavior as superstition on the part of the pilgrims. I see it as part of the great gift exchange between heaven and earth, the exchange between God and man, which takes place precisely on this level. The Cross of Jesus, after all, was man's worst attempt to prevail over divine goodness, and yet it was also God's greatest desire and God's greatest success in giving himself generously to us.

The hospitality the Copts afford the monk, which at once delights him and offends him, seems to me, then, to have both the element of genuine generosity and the Paschal Mystery enfolded into it, both at the same time. The Copts know they are being offensive on one level, but they are filled with so much joy, knowing that even by human offense, they are obtaining grace. *"O felix culpa*, O happy fault," we say in the Latin Church. In the offense of the Cross, the love of God was engaged by man for our blessing, our forgiveness, and our salvation.

### Apocalyptic Resignation

DECEMBER 6, SATURDAY

In my discussions with the monks and with the pilgrims who come here, I have no doubt that, secretly, in the deepest places of their soul, the Copts have preserved the missionary spirit of the Christian Church and that, therefore, they cannot but hope for a Christian Egypt. It's a poignant thought. They are a small minority: ten to fifteen percent at most, and for purposes of denigration, they are accounted as fewer. They are silenced; they are muted. They are unable to politicize their needs or to obtain recourse for the injustices done to them. And yet that they should hope that they might somehow be a leaven in their society and draw it in a new direction is very touching. They hope for this, not only because they would be free of the onus of being a minority, but also because they would joyfully share their Faith with the majority of the nation. Of course, such a hope on their part is vital to the integrity, the authenticity of their spirituality if it is to be truly Gospel-oriented. I can see that it lives itself out in a variety of ways.

The great apparitions of the Virgin Mary in Zeitoun and more recently in Shubra and in other places in Coptic areas are certainly part of this almost eschatological hope. The return of the relics of St. Mark to the cathedral by the last Patriarch, and even the special circumstances under which Pope Kyrillos ascended to the throne of St. Mark, followed later by Pope Shenouda, give rise to their hope. The revitalization of their monasteries, their parishes, their studies, their language: all of these things presage for them the possibility of a new era. If these things can happen, then their quiet hope is that other, even greater, things can also happen.

The Copts are by no means foolish; they are aware that all around them in Egypt and in all of the Arab world beyond there is a tremendous rise in the intensity and the powerful advocacy of Islam. They know that, while there are certain promising signs in their midst, there are also contradictory signs. They are, therefore, in a certain kind of vise; they are squeezed between rising hopes and rising fears. They are squeezed between a great Gospel missionary desire on the one hand, and great dread on the other. In fact, Islamicism threatens their very existence.

The risings of hope and fear together are the recipe of the religious attitude of expectation called "apocalyptic." The Copts believe that God has a plan, but this plan will come about only by almost pyrotechnical, otherworldly displays, by cosmological wrenching. They do not know how much suffering it will entail, but they do not imagine, as apocalyptic people in the West often do, that this will happen in a triumphal way. They imagine that God will bring about great things through trials and travails, through the Paschal Mystery of his people participating more and more deeply in the drama of the Cross. So the question they must naturally ask themselves is: "How much suffering will it entail?" And the answer they must always give is: "Not more than we are able to endure." They will not be tested beyond their strength. The trouble is that their ancestors often had to evidence great strength, sometimes even unto martyrdom.

In the end, the Copts believe that the Apostolic See of Alexandria will be reestablished as a see of preeminence, and that everyone will recognize and honor it. Though much maligned nowadays for their backwardness and ineffectiveness, the Copts believe that the See of Alexandria will one day be universally esteemed. They believe that their liturgy will one day be chanted everywhere, alongside the other great liturgies of Christendom. They believe that Africa, in particular, will come to faith and will be seen as the spiritual province of Alexandria. They believe that the rest of Christendom will look to the See of Alexandria for her spirituality, for her devotion and her worship, and that even Moslems will yield to her gentle sway.

To their credit, the Copts have almost never permitted their apocalyptic zeal to surface in acts of rioting or in hostilities, or even in popular discourse. The jokes that they occasionally whisper, which touch upon themes of Muslim and Coptic relations, are always told in a secular vein. They never permit their religion to be enlisted to provoke violence. Their genuine anguish, their suffering under so much oppression, mutes the public speaking, even the communal speaking, of their apocalyptic hopes amongst themselves. These things are mostly unsaid, but if you probe, if you ask, if you gain their confidence, they begin to tell you about them. In fact, I've never seen such resignation on a collective level before. I've seen individuals who are resigned to fate, to illnesses, to familial situations that are unsolvable. I've seen individuals who are resigned to God's will, but I've never seen a whole people with such a collective gentleness, such a communal mentality of quiet martyrdom and great serenity as that which the Coptic people evidence as they place themselves in the hands of God.

The Copts can speak, even tearfully, about being driven into the desert, in much the same way that Islamicists have compelled the Jewish nation to think about being driven into the sea. But they have far less opportunity to protect themselves than Israel does, so they speak with resignation and sorrow—not so much about themselves as individuals, but about others. When a woman speaks about her mother being a part of that great suffering, or a man speaks about his wife, or when children speak about their parents, then they show their emotions. But the emotion is one of sorrow, not of anger, and very rarely and much less is it an impulse leading to any strategy as to what they can possibly do about it.

The Copts believe that great suffering is the place where the kingdom of God settles upon the earth, that the Cross, after all, is the axis around which the kingdom turns. It was on the Cross of Jesus, they point out to me, that he was announced as King, the

King of the Jews, by the sign inscribed above him. It will be the people who are willing to embrace the Cross communally around whom the kingdom will one day unfold. They see themselves as the Church Suffering, the Church Martyred and, therefore, the place where the kingdom of God will be built upon earth.

In all their Marian apparitions, when the Virgin appears, however luminous or indistinct, she never speaks. She only weeps, or she looks sadly, lovingly, and silently on her children. It's actually very moving. When she doesn't speak, she honors the Coptic people who cannot speak. Though she moves their hearts and looks at them with a certain palpable power of persuasion, she doesn't raise her voice because there is no voice now for them to raise. They must move as Jesus moved, as a lamb led to the slaughter, meekly, opening not his mouth. They must suffer silently, like Mary as she is so often portrayed in the Gospels, following the steps of her Son—most especially along the way of his Cross. They must also pray silently, as Mary (from whom no word is quoted) did in the Upper Room. Mary is the still, quiet place in the middle of the Church from which prayer goes up in the Spirit of Jesus. So the Copts, likewise, see her as the secret, silent center of their community, of their nation, which, while having no voice, nevertheless, is able to pray with great power, great intercession, and great praise. *Fiat et Magnificat.*

## DECEMBER 8, MONDAY

> *O Providential Father,*
> *The Apostle tells us, "...you do not know about tomorrow. What is your life? For you are a mist that appears for a little while and then vanishes. Instead, you ought to say, 'If the Lord wills, we shall live and we shall do this or that'"* *(James 4:14-15).*
> *Often I have asked you for the grace to guard me from presumption, to preserve me from the folly of vain boasts whereby I would assert assurances of the future and my plans in it. The future is wholly yours, and every plan of mine is the merest provision. I am the thinnest vapor, a passing mist. One blast of wind, one shaft of light, one cloudless nighttime chill, and I am gone. May I rest upon your world as a grate-*

*ful guest in the bounty of my gracious Host. Let not my tran-
sience make me desperate or thoughtless, hardened or distracted. Your breath, after all, gave this mist its power to live
in me. Let me breathe my prayer of praise to you. You have
answered my prayers and brought me to a land where every
voice acknowledges your sovereignty over the future. "In sha'
allah!" they speak one to the other at every turn.*

*Now I can feel the truth of the words: "In sha' allah: as
God wills." The desert sun itself dispels—devours—the morning mist at once, and before your face our plans and projects
are even less substantial vapors! Now I can obey the apostle's
injunction: "You ought to say, 'If the Lord wills...'" To be a
stranger in a strange land makes the force of this command
felt. Is this why you call your children away into the wilderness, up to the mountain, across the sea, or to a retreat?*

*I know all the details of how my journey fell out; my own
hand was in it from the start. But your hand was on mine,
and in the making of this journey I have always had the sense
of obeying your will for me. So I go on here in peace, not
knowing anything but that the future is yours and that I am
a fugitive on the earth just a little while. This momentary
resignation makes me quiet and glad. You are God, and my
journey is yours to direct, through Christ Jesus, your Son.
Amen.*

## Green Cards

DECEMBER 12, FRIDAY

Sometimes it seems that every young Egyptian is interested in
somehow getting an American visa or a green card, or at least a letter of recommendation from someone who can help him get one.
Everyone is interested in obtaining a job contact or a scholarship
or a referral, or even finding someone who is marriageable, so that
by one of these means he can go to the United States. It seems that
everyone, especially under a certain age, is desperate to get out of
the Third World, to get out of Egypt as it is.

I hear these requests from pilgrims, from parents for their children, from monks for members of their families, from employees
of the monasteries, from Copts all over, and even from Moslems!

Everyone seeks the assistance of "his" American, and there is always the hope that maybe they have been blessed, that the one to whom they are speaking is connected well enough to get them out. It is very burdensome, very tedious, to always be in a position where I find myself unable to assist them. They don't accept the fact that I am not able to help them. They imagine that I am simply being difficult or stubborn, that I am protecting my own interests, or that I am disdaining their entreaty. And so they pursue. They hound; they knock, ever louder, at the door.

I'm always trying to persuade these people that it is not a panacea to go to the United States. It's not the solving of all problems; it's not the pleasure of all pleasures to live in that country. But they don't believe me. They imagine that I am somehow trying to keep the number of seekers and finders away, that I'm trying to diminish the number of those who share in the bounty.

So, for these reasons, I have accepted an invitation to go back to Cairo from the desert to attend a party to be held by one of the members of the American embassy. The attaché and his wife host a party from time to time to which they invite transplanted Americans who are living in Egypt. I had not imagined that I would ever go. I can almost remember thinking that I would not accept the invitation I received when I first appeared at the embassy to confirm my visa for a longer period of stay. I put it out of my mind. But now that the date for that party is coming up, I think that I shall go after all because perhaps I might be able to make a contact there who would be able to help one or another of the people who entreat me for assistance.

So I returned to Cairo this evening, and went to the attaché's home where I was greeted by his peers. They were curious as to what I am doing in Egypt. They saw my habit, of course, and when I explained that I am staying in the desert monasteries, I could see that they were intrigued. "Isn't it a dying Church," they asked, "filled with superstition?" "Aren't they all anti-intellectuals who live out there in the desert?" "An antique collection," someone said. "Besides, isn't it the most disorganized of all religions?" This is how they described the Copts.

They tried to appeal to my sense of being an American who would disdain the Islamic or the Arab world with all its complexities. Or they appealed to me, they thought, in terms of my being a *Roman* Catholic who would appreciate the good order of an ecclesiastical bureaucracy over the chaotic and discordant institution of the Coptic Church. They tried to appeal to me as a *Western* monastic, one trained in apostolic service to the Church and the larger world around it, as opposed to what, they thought, is the non-life-giving or the inward-looking monasteries of the Coptic religious community. In all of this, they were seeking my agreement. Could I not agree with them? Could I not condescend with them? Of course, their perspective was neither monastic nor Catholic, nor even especially Christian. They simply assumed what my perspective might be.

It was something of a crisis for me, because if I disagreed, I thought, then they might never help me should I come back to them later with an entreaty from someone wanting to go to the States. If I angered them, if I embarrassed them by my disagreement, or spoke against their point of view, they would simply dismiss me and anyone whom I brought to their attention. On the other hand, if I agreed with them, not only would I lose my own integrity, but their own lack of respect for the Copts would be reinforced. In the end, I suppose that that was the critical thing. If their disrespect could be any greater, they wouldn't care to help them much anyway. So I decided to disagree.

I told them that I do not think the Coptic Church is dying. I think there is a kind of genius in its lack of organizational strategies which makes it less vulnerable to those who might be more likely to attempt to suppress a highly efficient, organized Church. I think the Coptic Church is a Church of great holiness, and that their monasteries are doing exactly what monasteries should be doing. Whether or not they are engaged in material, apostolic service is not so important. The essential thing is the interior, internal prayer life of the monastery and its witness. That's what matters most.

I could see that the wife of the attaché, who herself is Catholic, was actually offended by what I had to say. Her non-Catholic husband, however, was more careful in his outward display. He arched his eyebrow at me, then found an opportunity to turn away, to be with others at the party. So I shrugged my shoulders and thought that all was lost. I had come back from the desert to this awful party, only to burn bridges behind me whereby I might have been of service to people who had asked for my help. Had I taken the moral high ground at their expense? How moral was that?

## December 15, Monday

Almost as a follow-up to my last visit, I traveled into downtown Cairo to the American embassy this morning with a young man named Emil. He wanted me to represent him to the attaché or the ambassador, to give him a letter of recommendation, and to speak on his behalf so that he might get a visa to go to the United States. I agreed to accompany him to the embassy because he so much wants to go, and because he and his family have been so hospitable to me whenever I have come back to Cairo from the desert.

I know that the embassy gives these visas to fewer than one in fifty of those who ask for them. The number dispensed to young unmarried men is even lower, because it is assumed that they will never return to Egypt, even if they arrive in the States with just a "tourist" visa. I explained this to Emil and his family. They understood, but they still wished us to go. So off we went to the horrors of Cairo's traffic and came to the embassy. We took our seats and waited for hours.

Finally, the attaché decided to see me before he saw Emil. I was invited in to his office. We spoke for a while. He asked me if I planned to go to the Monastery of St. Catherine in Sinai. I told him that I expect to go there eventually. He reached under his desk and gave me a bottle of brandy to give to the abbot. He explained that he realizes this is a Greek Orthodox monastery, but he knows the abbot of the monastery and he wishes to send him a gift, even if the abbot uses it only for "the occasional thirsty guest." I agreed to take it. He made no reference to the young man I had brought to the embassy. He made no reference to the letter of recommendation that I wrote for Emil. I spent ten minutes with him in pleasantries and took my leave.

A few minutes later Emil was called into his office and came out in no time at all with a visa! The attaché said to him, "I know you will try not to return to Egypt when you enter the United States, but I may give a visa to whomever I choose, and I choose to give one to you!" I was quite surprised at the attaché's attitude. I have no assurance that this will continue, but at least this once he was accommodating. Apparently, he does not disdain the Copts, nor apparently did he even disdain my defense of them. He has his own wits and his own ideas, and he chose, in this case, to open a door.

## A Coptic Family

When we returned to Emil's home, his parents broke into tears, both in joy for their son who will be able to live in the United States (a dream that many have) but, of course, also a joy tinged with sorrow because they will lose him to a great distance.

Emil comes from an interesting family. His father and mother are first cousins; their parents were also first cousins. They all lived in a village in Upper Egypt in which the Christians are few in number. Since the draw from which they could marry was relatively small, it became the custom there to prefer to marry one's cousin. As a result, the Kamal-Hanna family told me that they have first cousins in their parental lines as far back as seven generations.

The Kamal-Hannas are very traditional Coptic. Their manner, their sense of family and lineage, of tradition, and of trust in Providence all speak of great stability. They're from an old lineage and, although they are by no means well off, they expect that every one of their children will marry into a good family. Rich or otherwise, it doesn't matter; wealth is not the issue for them. The issue is the strength of the family, its solidity, and the character that strong families create.

Emil's mother, Madame Juliet, has a French name and was French-taught in one of the Catholic schools in Cairo. Emil's father speaks English because he was taught in an English-speaking Catholic school. The Coptic families, if they could at all afford it, sent their children to Catholic schools. Consequently, in many Coptic homes, the wife speaks French in addition to Arabic, and the husband speaks English in addition to Arabic. This dual language pattern appears to be a mark of polite society.

When I am visiting the home of the Kamal-Hannas, Madame Juliet always attempts to speak to me in French. She cannot really believe that an educated American, an educated priest, cannot speak French. So I try to make do. I try to figure out what she is saying from the etymologies of the few Latin bases I know. She is especially interested in hearing me sing any parts of the old Mass that I know, because when she attended the Catholic school as a child, she fell in love with the Tridentine Mass. I know some parts of the *Missa de Angelis* and I sing the *Salve Regina* from the Office for her. She is delighted! An older woman, she takes great pleasure in recalling these memories of her childhood.

Her house is open and hospitable to many. The Kamal-Hannas are a family famous in the region among the Christians, and even among the Moslems, for their hospitality and graciousness. They are extravagant in their generosity, according to the customs of the old ways.

Emil's parents threw a party for him that evening and many people came to offer their congratulations. There were several women working in the kitchen. One of them, I noted in particular, is Muslim. She was brought in for the occasion because many guests were expected. She pulled me into the kitchen for a moment to show me a rosary in her purse. She explained to me that she loves Mary and she loves Christians and that she wishes she had somehow been raised in a Christian country. Then her husband would not divorce her, or threaten to divorce her, she said. I did not have the heart to tell her that, in so-called "Christian" countries, divorce is very common. But among the Copts in Egypt it is not; it is strongly, strongly discouraged. So Muslim women often admire the relative peace of the Christian wife who is not intimidated by the threat of divorce. That alone, the Muslim woman said, makes the Christian wife the equal of her husband.

The well-wishers came to congratulate Emil, one after the other, and they expressed their thanks to me. Quite a few of them were even more excited at the thought that I might help them or their family members get to the United States as well. The pressure to spirit people to America only increases as a result of this initial success. Alas!


## Of Rock Concerts and Papal Audiences

DECEMBER 17, WEDNESDAY

I went off this evening to the Cathedral of St. Mark in Cairo where Pope Shenouda was giving his Wednesday evening conference to the youth of the city. Thousands of young people come for this weekly audience with the man they call "our Pope." He stands on a platform, or he sits on a large chair, answering questions they have placed in a box. For an entire hour and a half he has them in the palm of his hand. They applaud him wildly. He has such charisma, and yet his answers are of the *most* traditional sort. He presents wholly and entirely the Orthodox teachings of his Church, in belief and in practice, in asceticism and inspiration. The youth of the city are completely overwhelmed by the power of his presentation, and they applaud him as though they were at a rock concert. So there is a certain incongruity to it all: all these young people attired (as much as they can be) in the fashions of their time, applauding a man wearing the ageless garments of a desert monk or an Oriental potentate. Pope Shenouda, like all the bishops and patriarchs of the Coptic Church, was a desert monk before he was elected. They are the only Copts who can become bishops in their Church.

After the conference, I made my way toward the papal residence through a rather thick throng of excited and happy young people. Many of them stopped me and asked me for my name and address: my address in the States. They wanted to know what I'm doing here. More requests for visas and green cards. What will I do?

I finally reached the papal residence where an attendant let me in, and I spoke to His Holiness for a few minutes that evening. He said that he'd be happy to take me with him the next day back to the monastery where he thinks I should be, or I think I should be. I was then ushered from his presence and escorted across the plaza near the cathedral to what is called the *Ghallesium*, that is, the house of Butros Butros Ghalli of the famous Ghalli family. One of the attendants provided a room for me there. Actually, it's more like a palace than a house. Apparently there is a cordial understanding between the Patriarchate and the Ghallise that certain guests of the Patriarch can be housed for a time in their mansion.

### Relations with Rome

DECEMBER 18, THURSDAY

In the morning I visited the library of the Société d' Archéologie Copte which is adjacent to the plaza of the Patriarchate. After spending a few hours there, I walked over to the offices of Pope Shenouda. Then I got into a car that was waiting for me. We drove to the desert from this point of departure, through the city of Cairo, past the pyramids of Giza, and onto the desert highway between Alexandria and Cairo. Several hours along on our journey, we took a road which veers off to the left and started our way to the Monastery of St. Bishoi.

Once we arrived there, His Holiness invited me to attend Vespers over which he was to preside in the papal residence adjacent to the monastery. After we prayed Vespers, I was taken to a hospitality room where I had supper. The only other guest there was a Coptic nun.

After the supper, the Pope sent for me and took me for a walk through the desert, near the perimeter of the monastery. As we walked, His Holiness spoke to me of his vision for ecumenical relations. Here, he told me that well-catechized high school students would be capable of resolving the difficulties between the Catholic and Orthodox Churches, except that history, politics, and ambition have forever clouded the issues that need to be agreed upon. "The faith is simple; a child can grasp it. The true Church is so simple in its unity of love in Christ."

Nevertheless, he said, he has anxieties about Catholicism in this respect: with which Catholicism should he reconcile? From what he has read, there are now several voices claiming to represent the Catholic Church, even about essential matters of doctrine. So how could he speak about a union or intercommunion between his Church and the Catholic Church when that might cause members of his Church to be scandalized or confused? They might imagine that he was negotiating with irreconcilable forces. I gather that he considers some of these "voices" to be irreconcilable with what he considers the true nature of the Catholic Church.

At any rate, I began to understand, not so much from what he said, as from the gravity of how he spoke, that if the Coptic Church were in some way aligned with worldwide Catholicism, it would suffer the great disadvantage of being reckoned as a foreign Church *in* Egypt, rather than a national Church *of* Egypt. There are already enough difficulties, the Pope said, in being the national Church of a Christian minority in an Islamic world. But to be a "plant" of a foreign, Christian power (Rome) would profoundly compromise the safety and integrity of his Coptic people. Yet the Pope spoke of their ecumenical relations, Coptic and Catholic, or Coptic and Islamic, with the greatest delicacy, perhaps from his years of cultivating the practical arts of religious diplomacy.

No, he said, Orthodoxy must find union first. First, the Orthodox Churches must discover their oneness. They must recover their apostolic unity and then, he said, on that basis, they could approach Catholicism from a position of relative confidence, even relative strength. In that position—not one of intimidation or threat—they might be able to summon Catholicism back to herself, to summon from the many voices that *one* voice which is hers and hers alone. By this means, they might be able to draw Catholicism back to her genuine authenticity and integrity, and make it a plausible voice in ecumenical relations once again.

## The Solar Disk and the Cross

As we spoke, the sun began to set. As we gazed at the beautiful sunset in the western desert, Pope Shenouda spoke rather poignantly about the role of the sun in the ancient Coptic and Egyptian world. He said that the ancient Egyptians worshiped the sun, Ra, but they saw it as a continuous cycle, repeating itself: a cycle of day and night, life and death, fertility. But we as Christians, he said, do not see it as a cycle which repeats itself. Rather, for us, it is a Paschal sign. It is not an endless circle of repetition, but a daily pattern of a mystery which has been fulfilled once and for all. It is the Paschal mystery that the sun evidences, he said, for it is blood red at night, representing the descent of God into human flesh and of Christ into the earth. The sunset represents the descent of God into the lowest parts of human suffering and even of human sin; his descent, through blood, into human death.

The sun rises in the morning as Christ rose in the morning, *"rejoicing like a champion to run his course"* (cf. Psalm 19:6). It rises in the morning as an image of a truth that was revealed in Christ: that human nature rises up in Christ to holiness.

The setting sun and the rising sun are complementary signs, the iconography of the Paschal Mysteries. Night, the Pope said, is essential to this diptych, to understanding the meaning of these two images, for one cannot distinguish a setting sun from a rising sun, except by the night between them.

So, he said, the history of the Coptic Church through the long night, and the history of each soul through so much suffering, are both poised between these two great signs. The one which is to come—the resurrection of our own bodies on the last day—is no less real than the one which has already past. Both have occurred, both are real in the body of Christ, both are true. The promise of our resurrection is not a promise of something yet to come, but the assurance of that which has already occurred: the Resurrection of Christ, which is our own source of life.

Such was the reflection of the Coptic Pope on the setting of the sun. On the one hand, he was presenting something remarkably Christian, something which had never been considered before: relating the sun to the Gospel. But, on the other hand, he was conjoining it to something quite ancient: the Egyptian meditation on the solar disk and its daily rotation. These two themes are entwined in the design of the Coptic cross. It is abstracted from the cruciform shape of the mode of Christ's execution and incorporates the Pharaonic *ankh*, the hieroglyphic "keys of life" taken from the ancient religion of sun worship.

## *Pilgrim Tours*

### DECEMBER 19, FRIDAY

I finally got back to my room in the monastery today, although Friday is not the most propitious day for retirement here. Friday is the Islamic day of rest and worship, so everyone in Egypt has off from their jobs. Friday is, therefore, the day when most of the tourists and pilgrims come to the monastery. They are here for various reasons. Some really are on tour, exploring the church and the many shrines on the monastery grounds. I give some of the tours to those who speak English, especially if they are foreign groups. Small groups come here occasionally, especially from Germany. I also give some of those tours in broken German.

There are those who are here for individual counseling, looking for spiritual direction, either because their director is here and they come regularly, or because they are in special need at this time in their life. There are people who come here for marriage counseling; there are those who come here to seek a monk's advice about finding a marriage partner. They hope that he may know someone who knows someone who can make a good arrangement for them. Of course, there are always those who come for blessings and for healings and for words of wisdom to guide them in their life. Not counseling, just a word: some insight that a monk can give them in a moment of grace.

Some are here for picnics. They really do come with baskets of food and they lay it out somewhere in the gardens or the plazas of the monastery. They spend the whole day just enjoying the blessing of being in a holy place. Of course, for many of them, it is such a great relief to be in a setting which is wholly and entirely Christian. They are putting down the burden of always being in someone else's land, in someone else's housing, under someone else's inspection. They feel like foreigners, strangers, never really at ease until they come to the monastery. Even in the churches of Cairo or the villages of the Delta, the Copts are surrounded by people who are outside the Faith. But here, in the otherwise empty desert, they are surrounded only by their peers, all of whom share a common Faith.

Some are here for catechesis, that is to say, they come in groups with their teacher who uses the art of the church and the icons in various shrines as teaching tools. Some are here because they have an architectural or archaeological interest in the role of the monastery through the long history of the Coptic Church, or as a continuation of ancient Egyptian architectural or artistic themes. An often overlooked fact is that the Copts are the true descendants of the original Egyptians, the people who built the pyramids and temples. And although they do not have the infrastructure to create structures on a scale as large or complex as those created by their ancestors, nevertheless, they are clearly their descendants. As such, they have maintained any number of pre-Christian and pre-Islamic traditions which are actually Pharaonic in their origins.

Some of the people who come are actually here for exorcisms. There is a line of them in the back of the church which I hadn't noticed at first. One of the monks, who is regarded as especially well equipped spiritually for this role, exorcises evil, demons, from a variety of people who come to him. I spoke to him about it once, and he explained that Christians can be what we might describe in English as "obsessed" by evil of various kinds. Non-Christians, the unbaptized, can actually be possessed by it. He blesses all who come and ask, so that they may be delivered of the evil, delivered by the power of the Paschal Mystery of Christ.

This is a dangerous charism, a dangerous vocation, the monk told me, because if he himself were much liable to doubt or to fear or intimidation, then these evils would be crafty enough to take hold of him and do him damage. But, he said, contrary to what people might think, it is not his holiness so much as simply the gift of faith which preserves him from this danger. So he goes about his day, at least on Fridays, performing many of these exorcisms.

Quite a few of the people who are in the line are not Christian at all. They come to the monasteries, especially in the evening—perhaps so as not to be easily recognized. They come because they feel that they are oppressed by evil. They say that their own sheiks do not deal with this kind of power, but only with the One God, so they appeal to the Christian monk instead. By this kind of explanation, they get the help they need, yet preserve a sense of their own religious integrity.

DECEMBER 20, SATURDAY

The weather has been cooling gradually throughout all of this month. Without any central heating or cooling, indeed, even without any strong doors to separate the inside from the outside, the weather on the inside is almost identical with that on the outside. At night, especially, there's quite a chill; the temperature drops to freezing.

All the monks seem to suffer more from the cold than from the heat. Egyptians, in general, seem to be better suited to the warmer climate. So the monks are attired in layer upon layer of scarves and capes or coats, many layers of socks and gloves and hats—all these on top of their habit, making some rather extraordinary crazy quilts of appearances! I have a trench coat, a London-Fog-like black coat that I wear over my habit, and I have black gloves. Everything I have is black. The monks look at me and I can almost hear them sniff that this is all a little too grandiose: that things should be so coordinated in a wardrobe for a monk! But they're polite, and I try not to show my interest in and amusement at the wild colors they are wearing: clothes from all manner of dress covering what is otherwise a very serious black habit.

## Coptic Rubrics

After morning prayer today there was no Kodes. Throughout much of Advent, the Coptic Mass has been moved to noon. Instead, the monks go right from morning prayer to their cells for meditation and reading. The reason that this shift has occurred is not because of Advent per se, I'm told, but because there are nearly a dozen men here who are learning to be proper celebrants, proper priests and presiders, and they are very busy in the mornings, studying the various rites of the Coptic Church. The monks who would otherwise be assisting at the Kodes are intensely occupied, teaching them the hymnody, the liturgical gestures, and the rubrics of the Coptic Eucharist.

It's an extraordinary thing, really. The average Coptic priest is simply commissioned by his church. The parishioners recommend the fellow to the bishop and the bishop takes their request under advisement and perhaps ordains the young man. Of course, this means that someone who is probably more or less worthy, someone who is devout and practical, has been ordained. But he is not necessarily someone who has had any prior training in Coptic sacramental rites or Coptic theology.

So, after ordination, these priests are bundled up and taken to a monastery where they literally spend forty days on retreat, spiritually consolidating the transition that has just occurred. They learn to celebrate the Coptic Kodes and the Coptic sacraments so they can officiate at these rites when they return to their parishes. They grow beards. Since every Coptic priest in the service of the Church, like every Coptic monk, grows a beard, it would be considered unseemly for a newly ordained priest to appear with a half-grown one. So forty days in a monastery after ordination gives them the opportunity to grow in religious knowledge, in the practice of religious ritual, and even to grow a beard. Of course, that is what Pope Shenouda also asked me to do when I first arrived.

All day long I can hear them practicing. They're in all the smaller chapels: the center ones and the side ones of the monastery church. They're also in the monastery keep which is not far from where I'm living, so I can hear them in the rooms which have been converted into chapels there. I can hear them praying and singing the various intonations of the Coptic Kodes. It's quite a lot to learn because the musical corpus is fairly substantial. There are several liturgies, in fact, which are proper to the Coptic rite, all of which the priests must know, as they are used in the various seasons of the year. Of course, there are also many variations in orations and prefaces for the saints' days and feasts, so the cycles are rather complex. There's a lot for the priests to study; it takes hours and hours a day. I think that some of these poor priests are actually rehearsing ten or twelve hours a day!

I feel particularly sorry for the Coptic monks who must teach them. It's a never-ending cycle of education for some of them. In a certain sense, they are "liturgical machines," constantly providing instruction for the many young men coming through. Of course, the monks are thoroughly imbued with their Mass. They live and breathe the words of it. The rubrics and the prayers are all part of their flesh by now, and they seem to be totally absorbed in what they are doing. I had not really expected that so many of the monks here would be so deeply invested, liturgically. Surely, that is what one expects in a Benedictine monastery, but in the desert of Egypt, I had imagined that the monks would be somewhat less interested in the study of liturgical rites. Quite the contrary. For very practical reasons, the monastery is the school of the Lord's service, and the newly ordained come here to learn the liturgical arts, the *Opus Dei.*

So I have somewhat followed suit. I was invited by Abuna Tadros to study Coptic prayer with him while the others are learning the Coptic Mass. So, day after day, I go to the library now, usually in the late morning, to spend a couple of hours studying Coptic vocabulary, even a little Coptic grammar, especially as it is used in Coptic prayer. This work of trying to understand their prayer form more literally is regarded by Abuna Tadros, and I suspect by other monks as well, as essential to my education in the monastic life.

We are using the psalms, of course; that is the best course of action, since I know the psalms already. From the English translation, or even from the Arabic, I can learn the meaning of the Coptic psalms fairly rapidly from just a few clues, a few words here and there. Even the shape of the verse sometimes helps me to understand what I'm saying or what I'm hearing. It's wonderful to learn this ancient variation of the psalms since, actually, the Coptic psalms are part of the ancient monastic heritage and would have been used by the early monastic founders as their primary means of prayer.

DECEMBER 23, TUESDAY

*O Lord of Joy,*
    *Christmas, ten thousand miles from home! How strange*
*for me, this snowless emptiness without the overpowering*

*commercial trappings of an American holiday! Even the day of Christmas will pass here soon, and no one will accord my feast its due, since the Christians here celebrate the birth of Christ two weeks later.*

*How deep is the well of emptiness I look into, I look up from! How sweet to be alone in this exquisite way, apart from all that is familiar, when most of the rhythms of my body would ordinarily seek the customary associations of seasonal, social enjoyments! I am adrift more and more. Almost the day itself—the 25th—could pass without my much noticing it. Maybe only the strangeness of realizing that fact makes me realize it anew. Somehow, I better understand how St. Benedict came not to know even the date of Easter when he dwelt in his cave, for all days become alike. All days partake of the "One Day" of Christ, the Day of his being "raised up" from his Cross to his Glory. All things become at once great asceticism and sweet delight in the same moment.*

## Of Children and Stars

DECEMBER 24, WEDNESDAY

Christmas Eve in the Western rite. I went through this day as through others, privately mindful that this is Christmas Eve in my Church, but certainly aware of the fact that for everyone else here, Christmas doesn't come until January 7. Their Christmas Eve, then, is January 6. So I made no reference to this; I made it merely a matter of my own private prayer.

In the afternoon, a bus arrived from Cairo carrying young people of various ages from the Church of St. Mark in Heliopolis. The older ones were taken on tours and given instructions by the monks. A handful of the very young ones were left in my care. So I took them on a walk through the monastery and then farther, outside the monastery, into the lands immediately adjacent to the farming estate of St. Bishoi. There is a little pond there which is filled with fresh water pumped out of the desert floor. There are actually fish in it which the monks sometimes catch so that they can serve their guests this desert delicacy. This little pond is a beautiful setting around which we can sit on the sand and watch the sunset.

The children—six, seven, eight years of age—were asking me questions, as they always do when they come from the cities to the monastery. They always ask more or less the same kinds of questions. They ask about heaven; about what it is like to see Jesus there. They ask about Mary and the saints. They ask questions about who God is and what God is like. They never tire of asking these questions and listening to my answers.

So the hours passed. We built a little fire as the sun set, and they took their place around it, continually probing, asking, talking away. I reminded them from time to time that it was getting late and that soon we must be going back. I knew their group is staying over tonight, and I wanted them to be in the custody of their elders and their peers sooner rather than later. But they kept insisting, "We have lots of time," they said. "It gets dark early; we can stay here longer, Abuna. Tell us more about Jesus."

So the hours pressed onward into darkness. This has happened before. The little fire was burning low and they kept talking away. They were now exhausted with their questions in the night air as it cooled. Thank God, today had been a warmer day than usual. As they lay down on the sand, they huddled together, and still they asked questions. They could hardly keep their eyes open, but they insisted that we linger longer. Some were stretched out beside me and in front of me. One or two heads were propped against my lap and, still, they were talking. I went on answering their questions until finally I answered one at such great length that most of them fell asleep.

So there I was, sitting by the dying fire, with all of these sleeping children around me. I looked at them in the starlight and the moonlight and was touched by the fact that they are so filled with faith, so innocently seeking God. This is the second time since coming here to Egypt that I have found myself in exactly the same setting, surrounded by young people asking questions and listening to answers, tiring themselves out into exhaustion and sleep. And, just as before, there is once again that stabbing realization that none of these are *my* children, that I shall never have children such as these to instruct and to teach.

I looked up at the sky on this beautiful, clear desert night. I thought to myself that I had never seen such an array of stars, so numerous and so bright. Then, of course, at this moment, the passage from the Book of Genesis came to mind where God said to

Abraham, *"Look up into the night sky and count the stars, if you can. Just so shall your descendants be"* (cf. Genesis 15:5). So there I was sitting, looking up at the night sky, knowing how impossible it is in the desert night to count the stars. And even while I was feeling the special poignancy of not having children, I suddenly realized that these children all around me are not only children of Abraham, but they are also mine as well. For I have instructed them in faith, and I have given them tonight a greater realization of their own religion, their own spirituality. I have placed them confidently in the presence of God.

I thought of the second part of God's injunction to Abraham, to try to count the sands on the shore. I was sitting on the sand bank of a little pond, and it was just as impossible to number those grains of sand. But just as Abraham was promised numerous descendants, I realized that so also would my descendants be if I am faithful in proclaiming God's word.

At length I roused the children and took them back to the monastery where I delivered them to their families and their guardians.

I returned quietly to my cell, and there at my door was a gift! The monks had *not* forgotten, apparently, that this is my Christmas Eve! Somehow, they had found a Christmas tree, an awfully scraggly one, to be sure, but a Christmas tree of any sort in the middle of the desert is almost a miracle. It is some kind of evergreen, and on it they pinned little stars made of paper, all of them white, obviously signs of the Christmas star.

For me, they are also reminders of the stars I had just seen in the desert sky, and the promise that was given to me through Abraham.

# ☀ JANUARY

## A TIME OF CELEBRATION

> *O Lord of Glory,*
>
> *Blessed are you in the making of every season and in the dispensation of a new year of grace! I thank you that I may pass this threshold of time in the stillness of a desert night, far from all revelry and every human diversion. So silent and deep, this darkness of a new year in the wilderness! I turn my ear a moment toward the city of man, and it is so quiet here that I can somehow imagine that I hear the parties and the music of their celebrations. May they have joy in their festivities, O Lord of Joy. But have mercy on their souls, for tonight I can also hear the tones of desperation in their shrill outcries. I hear the wailing in their laughter. I even hear the shrieks of demons in the tumult and the din of drunkenness. Mercy, mercy, O Lord on us; mercy on me, who passes into this new year with the burden of all my own weaknesses, faults, and needs! Slip into our groans by the intercession of your good Spirit, the secret prayer of our yearning for you. For this I pray in Christ Jesus' name. Amen.*

### Christmas in the Coptic Orthodox Church

JANUARY 6 AND 7, TUESDAY AND WEDNESDAY

Tuesday evening into Wednesday morning. Throughout the day, yesterday and today, the monks were quieter than usual, if that

86

can be imagined. The emphasis was on intense Scripture reading, the rationale simply being that the Word is made flesh in Christ Jesus at Christmas. Or, at least, at Christmas the Word is revealed to our eyes in Christ Jesus who was born into the world that day. So the monks gave their eyes over to the reading of Scripture all day long.

On Christmas Eve at 3:00 P.M., the monks assembled in the church and began the chanting of the pre-Christmas Office, the preparation for the Christmas Kodes at midnight. Actually, that service went from 3:00 P.M. until 9:00 in the evening. The Office included the chanting of special hymns, of special psalm tones and special readings. Lots of incensations, so there was a joyful atmosphere in the church.

Once again, pilgrims came from Upper Egypt and from Cairo and poured into the monastery. The church was filled with them. They trickled in all day, and by evening the church was packed. There was hardly enough room for the people to do what they usually do throughout the night—they will rest, they will be seated, or they will lie down on the floor. Once again, it will be a very familial, intimate liturgical assembly that passes the night, half-waking, half-sleeping, in worship.

After the preparatory pre-Christmas Office was sung, the assembly moved into the heart of the Eucharistic worship which continued from 9:00 P.M. until about 7:00 A.M. It was a Kodes similar in many ways to their other liturgies. There were several prefaces and orations and a special canon which are used only a few times during the year for their highest feasts.

### Bread for Pilgrims

As we were leaving the church at 7:00 in the morning, the abbot—whom they informally call their *kommos*—Anba Serabamon, handed me a large loaf of homemade bread, the kind which is otherwise used only for Eucharistic worship. It can, by extension, also be used for a blessing. Because the crowd was so great, he also gave a number of these loaves to other monks. The people will be hungry and they will be seeking blessings. On Christmas Day, the blessing should be not just words and an extension of the hand-cross or a touch; it should also be a chunk of bread, the monks told me.

Everyone, it seems, is mindful of the fact that the word "Bethlehem" means "House of Bread" and that the Word which is made flesh is also our food, our bread, our staff of life. So now on this day a great deal of bread was being handed about, back and forth, as people extended the life of Christ, the face of Jesus, to one another in the exchange of gifts, especially the gift of bread.

In proper fashion, one doesn't just take the bread that is offered. One bows to it and kisses the hand that holds it, so that the first taste is not of the bread, but of the hand extending it. As the monks explained, it is the person of Christ who is being kissed in the person who is holding the bread, and it is the substance of the heart of Christ that is being offered under the appearance of bread.

## The Christmas Feast

On Christmas Day, a festive meal was served which was the finest meal that I have seen so far in a desert monastery. There were cold chicken legs, chicken-fat broth, lamb cubes, rice, and two tangerines per monk—an extraordinary feast. The Coptic monks are, by and large, essentially vegetarian, not because of moral sensibilities regarding animal flesh, but in the spirit of ascetical sacrifice. They eat meat on the great feasts of Easter and Christmas, and do so with great relish. I didn't see anyone who seemed squeamish about it. To them, it is just as much an exercise of their spirituality to enjoy the feast as it is to endure the fast. In both cases, they are doing something joyfully for God. It is an expression of their orientation toward the mysteries of Christ's life and love.

## Of Christmas Treats and Fellowship

On Christmas morning, the abbot of the monastery of Deir Anba Bishoi led all the ambulatory monks on a walk. We walked across the desert floor to the nearby monastery of Deir el Suriani where the two assemblies gathered for Christmas greetings and conviviality. In the desert where, traditionally, the monks were solitary and isolated and pilgrims could not come in such great numbers, there was scarcely a new face to be seen for weeks, months, or even years on end. But on Christmas Day, the monks walked out of their monastery and visited another House. So there was this extraordinary exhilaration of being in a new context, of talking to people who have a different experience of life (if that can be said of monks living in different monasteries in the middle of the Sahara Desert). The monks were totally animated by the opportunity to speak to people they had not spoken to, in most cases, since their last assembly meeting on Christmas Day.

And, of course, there was the giving of gifts: little favors that monks had made from paper or from cardboard, decorations of a sort for Christmas Day. There were gifts of little food packages—cookies or tarts or chocolates—gifts that monks had received from pilgrims and saved to give to other monks on this festive occasion. There was a great drinking of tea of many kinds, not just the ordinary, daily teas, but teas with various spices, especially *karkadee*, a special concoction of southern Egypt which, I'm told, is good for nerves, especially for people who haven't slept for a while, for people who have been keeping vigils.

When this festive occasion came to an end, we walked back to our monastery. After an hour or two, we were greeted by a similar contingent from the same place from which we had come. The monks from Deir el Suriani now made their traditional walk to St. Bishoi, and the whole process was begun again. Several more hours of dialogue, several more hours of drinking teas and eating chocolates. The whole morning and afternoon of Christmas Day was given over to this wonderful exchange of greetings and joyful celebration.

I'm grateful that I had read enough literature on the subject of Egyptian and Coptic culture to have brought with me a bag of my own favors to distribute throughout the year. It was heavy and problematic enough to cart from the airports in the States and on the desert journey, but now it has come in handy: holy cards, pens, rosaries, little icons. They are nearly running out by now, but they have served me well as part of this diffusive exchange. I suspect that, without anything at all, I would still have fully shared in it. The monks are magnanimous, and don't seem to count or to record debts. Nevertheless, I feel more like a welcome participant by being able to occasionally offer something to those who are so generous in offering gifts to me. Is this a foretaste of the "economy" of grace in heaven?

## *A Holiday Visit*

On the evening of January 7, I received an invitation from the Kamal-Hanna family in Cairo to join them for some post-Christmas days of rest and recreation. This invitation came to me by hand-delivered mail from a Coptic taxi driver, who had driven pilgrims across the desert for this feast. He located me and handed me the letter. He obviously knew its contents, since he waited for me to return with him this evening. I would not have done so, except that this family is acquainted with the Pope and the letter indicated that it was the wish of Pope Shenouda himself that I should visit Cairo to see the Church from the other side: to see the manner of Coptic worship, the Coptic spirituality of the laity in the city of Cairo itself. Apparently, he trusts this family to be able to give me a fair, not to say positive, view of all things Coptic in the urban setting of Egypt. So I packed a bag and made my departure just as the sun was setting. We drove a while through the night, when there is less traffic on the desert highway, and arrived in the flat of the Kamal-Hannas in Heliopolis sometime after midnight.

## *A Formal State Occasion*

JANUARY 8, THURSDAY

I didn't really go to bed, with the night leading into this morning. There were many people in the home of the Kamal-Hannas who were watching television. Apparently, this is the one time of year when a Coptic event is covered by the media, that is to say, the government permits Christmas in the Coptic Church to be aired on TV in Egypt. So the Christmas Kodes celebrated by the Coptic Patriarch, Pope Shenouda III, is televised in the Coptic Cathedral of St. Mark in Cairo.

Of course, it is an extraordinary event, especially since everyone is aware that the Copts are, at best, a marginalized minority. At worst, they are a despised minority in Egypt. Even though everyone is aware that they suffer varying degrees of persecution, yet on this occasion, the media and the government treat the Copts in public fashion as though they were esteemed members of the society.

Here in the cathedral, the Coptic Patriarch presided over a congregation which included several of the heads of state of Egypt and her neighbors. Muslim sheiks and professors from Ain Shams and El Azhar Universities were present, as well as diplomats who are living in the vicinity of Cairo. Even President Hosnia Mubarak and his wife were there, both smiling, both dressed for a formal occasion of state here in the Cathedral of St. Mark. This is, in part, a pretense of "legitimating" the Copts on the part of the government to try to persuade Christian nations that here in Egypt there is a minority which is permitted to exercise its religion with tolerance, and even with appreciation, by the Muslim majority. So it is partly a diplomatic coup that once a year or so there is a kind of proper government and media outreach to the Coptic minority.

But it even seems to be a little bit more than that, as the family gathered around the television explained to me. When Pope Shenouda was released from house arrest, where he had been kept in exile in the desert monasteries for several years, the throng which turned out to welcome him in Cairo was so large (and jubilant) that it exceeded the number of Christians who actually live there. It certainly exceeded in style of celebration the kind of public profile the Copts wish to present. So they were certain that there were many Moslems present who are not sympathetic to Christianity in any way, but who were, nevertheless, glad to have the Pope return to his ancient See.

The reason for this, my friends explained, is that the people of Egypt realize intuitively that the office of the Patriarch is significantly older than any other office in Egypt. It is the only institution whose roots reach back through the Islamic into the Byzantine Period, and even further back into the Roman era. Remarkably, the office of the Patriarch of Alexandria, in some sense, even preserves traditions older than Christianity itself. At one point in the history of Egypt, the Patriarch of Alexandria inherited the rights and prerogatives of the governors of Egypt under the Romans. The governors of Egypt were actually the descendants of the last Ptolemaic Pharaohs of Egypt.

So, by a certain convoluted, indirect reasoning, the Coptic people and even many Moslems consider the Patriarch of Alexandria to be an extension of the Pharaonic dynasty. As such, the Patriarch provides a kind of anchor for the ethnic people of Egypt.

Almost the whole orientation of their heritage revolves around the axis of that office. When the Pope celebrates the Christmas Kodes, many other people besides the Christians take an interest in it because it is the exercise of an office which gives definition to the antiquity of the whole nation. It celebrates their roots, in all its various layers, reaching far back into their past.

When the Pope was in exile, the people of Egypt seemed to miss having this aspect of their heritage made visible. They were grateful to have him back. My friends tell me that the Egyptians like to punctuate their public life from time to time, especially at Christmas and again at Easter, with occasional references to the Patriarch and his office, and therefore to the Coptic people who gather around him.

## Of Monks and Sheiks

JANUARY 9, FRIDAY

I spent the morning in the library of the Société d'Archéologie Copte near the cathedral. In the afternoon I visited the hotel of a certain Mr. Tewfik, the owner of the Hotel Beirut in Heliopolis. Emil, one of the sons of the Kamal-Hanna family, is employed there, and he wanted me to meet his Coptic employer. Mr. Tewfik wishes to provide some means of transportation for me when I am traveling to and from the monasteries. He seems to be a very devout Christian and wishes to make some of his resources available for my work.

While I was in the hotel, I was introduced to two brothers, two Muslim young men. One of them, Hamid, asked to meet me because of some problems in his house that he wishes me to address. Mr. Tewfik and Emil left the room so that the two brothers could speak to me frankly. It seems that their father died some months ago. He had been living in the house, and since his death, they feel most uncomfortable, especially in the room where he died. They are sure that something is amiss in the house. Things are going wrong; things are getting lost; things aren't working; and people are having nightmares. "Frankly, there is a bad spirit in the house," they finally said, and they asked me to come and to bless it.

I was puzzled about the request and reminded them of something they should have already known, that I am a Catholic priest. They are Moslems and there seems to be a certain incongruity in their asking me to come to their house for such a ritual purpose. Nevertheless, they said that this is perfectly acceptable. Christian priests regularly make themselves available for such things as this—or at least some of them do. They said that I shouldn't be hesitant, and that I shouldn't be afraid that any problems would result. They wanted me to do this because they knew that I am not only a priest, but also a monk, and they especially like monks to give blessings.

Mr. Tewfik later explained to me quietly that, when they are invited to give such blessings, Christian priests don't interpret this as a special, secret vote of confidence from Moslems. Such things are not encouraged in Egypt, but they are permitted by Islamic practice. Moslems rationalize that priests are more involved with commerce regarding "lesser spirits" by their very nature as Christian priests. The Muslim sheik, on the other hand, is dealing with God directly, so he doesn't concern himself with such things. They say, "If you want to resolve a problem with evil spirits, you need someone whose religion is of a 'lesser sort.'" Using this explanation, Moslems feel free to invite monks or priests to come to their homes for special blessings. This perception is also evidenced when Moslems come discreetly to the monasteries for exorcisms.

So this evening, I was picked up by the two brothers and taken to their house where a great deal of food was served. Although I had eaten dinner and was satiated, nevertheless it is apparently essential to the process of the blessing that the one who comes be lavishly hosted. They are able to receive from him the gift he is giving only because they are, in fact, exchanging with him a gift of complementary or analogous value.

So, a great assortment of sweets and a wide selection of foods were provided, at a great deal of expense. There was a great deal of laughter and joking and storytelling—all of this on the subtext of my coming for the blessing. But it was an essential choreography whereby they opened themselves to receive the blessing they most desired from me. I realized that the blessing could not be something pro forma. It had to be something engaging, of a duration and an intensity that permitted them to receive its full value morally, as well as spiritually. After all of the food and all of the partying, the sons demonstrated their ability in playing music and performing Arabic dances. Then, finally, I asked that we might now proceed to the ritual blessing for the deliverance of the house from every shadow of evil.

I blessed water in their presence; I added salt to the water and they were very happy about that. I prayed several prayers in Latin; that especially pleased them. I sprinkled the holy water about profusely. I had no hesitation now in invoking the name of Jesus, in invoking the Paschal Mysteries. About this they seemed to have no difficulty. I liberally splashed holy water in the room in which the father had died, and splashed the family gathered there for prayer. Taking a piece of chalk, I wrote the house blessing signs over the lentils of their doors. I sang the *Salve Regina* and read a passage from Scripture. The whole blessing lasted fifteen or twenty minutes. They were very, very gratified. Near the end of the blessing, I could tell that they were emotionally fulfilled and spiritually confident. So I was able to bring closure to the little ceremony and make my farewells.

This was my evening's occupation. I got back to the Kamal-Hannas very late, but I was satisfied that an ecumenical gesture had been afforded to strengthen the respect between the Copts and the Moslems. Or, at least I hope so!

## Homecoming

### JANUARY 14, WEDNESDAY

In the morning, availing myself of the resources of Mr. Tewfik and the Hotel Beirut, I was taken by taxi from the flat in Heliopolis where I had been staying and driven directly down the desert highway back to the monasteries of the Wadi Natroun. I stopped briefly at Deir el Baramous and visited with Abuna Lucas, the guest master there whom I have met from time to time, and I viewed some of the archaeological excavations that are presently going on in and around the monastery. By late afternoon I was taken by the same taxi driver, who had waited all day, back to Deir Anba Bishoi.

At the Monastery of St. Bishoi, I was received very well by the monks, who said that they had missed me during these past days. So there was much tea to be drunk and Christmas chocolates were brought out. There was much discussion about how life had been for me in the city, how I had visited the Patriarchate and a variety of the churches in Cairo, and what my opinions of them were. They're all very happy that I'm getting more and more exposure to their Church and to their ethnic community. They are pleased that I am able to report favorably about everything that I have experienced.

It seems that the longer I stay here, the more important it is to many of the monks that my impression be a favorable one, that I will be able to report good information, and to report it positively. They know by now that there are any number of things I have observed that I could report in a less than favorable fashion, if that were my intention. But I think they are growing in confidence that my intentions are honorable in their regard. They are becoming more and more forthcoming, less idealistic in what they express to be the case of their Church and their monastery. They now feel they can rely upon my good intentions toward them.

## The Winter of Faith

JANUARY 21, WEDNESDAY

The desert is extremely cold now. I'm continually surprised at how cold the climate can become in the Sahara. I hadn't imagined how much more I would suffer from the discomfort of the cold than from the heat. That, in fact, has so far been the case here. By January, the sun can only warm for an hour or two of the day, and sometimes not even that much. There has been an overcast complexion to the skies these last few days. Waterless gray clouds deprive the surface of the desert of solar heat, the little bit that there is. So I'm more and more confronted with a paradox that I hadn't expected: the cold Sahara.

Of course, there is a certain joy in this, because I feel more immediately in touch with the earth and its seasons here, in the colorless Sahara Desert, than I felt in the States, where I am able to exercise a greater control over the comfort and discomfort of the seasons. There, the ranges of temperature are even more modest; the discomforts, at least, are more reduced. That is, I can turn on the air conditioner there, or I can turn up the heat. I can manage the controls in the car, my office, or my room. I can turn the hot water faucet up or down in the sinks, showers, and bathtubs. I can add more ice to my Cola, or reheat my coffee. I can even jump into a pool. The possibilities of escaping the discomforts of the seasons are all greater there.

I find myself in the unusual condition of being unable to cry out against the discomforts around me. Everyone here is experiencing them in more or less the same way, and I would feel foolish, even ridiculous, complaining about them. Besides, the complaint would get me nowhere; there are no solutions to these problems. This situation is unfamiliar to me and it is humbling. It is also unusual for me to live in the company of people who don't cry out and who don't complain, but who quietly and almost without thought accept these conditions.

Maybe one of the reasons my generation feels itself at such a distance from the generations that have gone before is because we don't occupy the world in the same way. We don't even occupy our skin in the same way. We are able to obtain more immediate consolations and comforts, and we deal less and less patiently with the eventualities afforded by nature.

But here, now, I consider that anything that brings me to a greater resignation, a greater submission to forces I cannot change, is also an opportunity for me to come into the presence of God whom I cannot control, and to acknowledge his sovereignty. I exercise no mastery over the will of God, but must come to a simple submission to it, a complete and peaceful acceptance of it. I can even extend this beyond the teachings of my own Faith to Judaism which certainly acknowledges a submission to God. Even the name "Israel" means the surrendering of oneself wholly and entirely to God's will. The name "Islam," likewise, has a similar meaning; Moslems also assert the value of submission to the will of God.

Now as I live in this Near-Eastern desert environment, I begin to taste something of the seasonal and climatic atmosphere in which Judaism and Islam, as well as Christianity, came to know the sovereignty of God, the almighty hand of God exercised through creation. Creation itself is a sign of the divine authority over all the heavens and the earth, the exercise of divine love by which heaven and earth came to be.

JANUARY 22, THURSDAY

> *Hidden Lord,*
>       *My crying out is to you, O God, to you! The prayer of my greatest needs rises up from the deepest place within me. How*

*else would I know this place, except that you permitted these needs by which I found it? I would have fled the vast emptiness of need and desire within me, but you have driven me out into the desert; driven me "in," to face you here. You have hidden yourself here as once Moses encountered you in the burning bush, or on the quaking mountain. Commonplace things are ablaze with your presence; the solid earth sways before you. Nothing is as it seems!*

*So, in this place, prayers rise up from depths more deeply than before. Always, en route, the heart that travels lonely stretches calls out at last to you above all. It was always you, Hidden Lord, to whom I was calling all along, although I did not realize it. Beyond the face I saw, behind the eyes which saw me, silent in the conversation shared, hidden in the hands which clasped, your form was revealed only when cloaked between the two who embraced. This desert around me swallows up all sound, all cries, and all prayers into its silence. You are listening, Lord, and at last I perceive it.*

### Desert Walks

JANUARY 23, FRIDAY

I took a walk again this afternoon, for several hours, through the desert. It is a pattern of behavior that I have adopted from the monks who live here. Those who are able to walk distances do so, it seems, almost every day. It is an interesting exercise because, no matter in what direction I walk, everything always looks the same. There are no features, no external signs to differentiate one path from another, or one kind of journey from another, from one day to the next. So it's always the same relentless monotony, of day to day and path to path.

It's very different from walking near my home monastery of St. Vincent. There, one path is dramatically different from another. One is open; you can see the mountains in the distance; you can see the ridge and the trees on the horizon. The other path is relatively enclosed. The trees are nearby; they form a canopy. The hillsides surround you when you walk through that path. There are buildings; there are semi-natural and orchard-like settings through which the path winds. Every day you can take a different path, and every day the external signs will always keep you interested.

Not here. It's all the same. While I am walking a great deal, I have no external stimulation to make the walk the occasion of my meditation. The emptiness, the barrenness, has the cumulative impact of driving me inward, making me reflective and introspective. But being so here is different than being reflective in my own country. Here, my reflection is easily prevented from becoming externalized. When I am meditating in my country, I can look about and find things all around me on which to affix my interior dispositions, on which to hang the thoughts that are inside me. There's nothing here onto which I can project the interiority of my soul.

The desert represents the province of God on the edges of the empire of men. But ultimately, for us, it represents the territorial claim that God has, even within the illusory claims made by men. And that's what I am slowly discerning as I walk through the desert: that in the end, the garden and the oasis, the farm and the orchard, all the watered lands of the earth are proximate to and prone to become a desert. The secret, hidden identity of the earth, wherever it is, is a desert locale.

In the second creation account in Genesis, God begins his creative work not in a watery chaos but in an earthly desert out of which he causes a spring to flow. I now see that unless God continually causes the springs of life to well up, all the world will eventually revert back to a desert. Every kind of territory, every kind of environment will become a desert almost overnight if certain vital, continuous forces are not brought to bear, such as the ongoing rain, the yearly floods of rivers, and the currents of wind that always bring climatic change and refreshment. Without the vital work of the Spirit, without the vitality that he brings to life through constant change and movement, the world would become a dead world, a desert world. God's authority over life and death, God's capacity to bring life, or not, is in a certain sense represented by the emptiness of the desert.

The desert is at once a threat because we cannot control it but, on the other hand, it generates great exhilaration because it puts us in the presence of the One whom we cannot control, the force which we cannot manage, the name which we cannot speak. It is a powerful means of placing us in the presence of God. It reminds us of our littleness, of our helplessness in the face of the Creator, even in the face of the created.

Abuna Elia told me some time ago that the desert has the power to empty us out. It draws out of us everything that is within us, not because we project into it, but because it drains us, it impoverishes us. In that sense, there's a certain kind of immersion that happens, a baptism. As the children of Israel had to learn to be baptized in water, which was for them a symbol of death, so, according to Abuna Elia, we must be immersed into the desert to learn our helplessness before the God who called us here. The desert imposes on us the iconography of his power.

Surely for the monk who lives in the desert, these meditations are spontaneous and daily affairs. So spontaneous, so natural are they that they make it possible for him to take a walk in the desert every day. For him, there is no gratification beyond the sentiments by which he enjoys the love of God, even in emptiness, even in poverty. Love for love's sake, rather than for the benefits which are gained: a walk through the desert, rather than a garden.

JANUARY 26, MONDAY

*Invisible God,*

*Blessed may you be forever for your eternal presence! Your ineffable purity and wordless love never strives nor strains. You are Rest without weariness, Peace without tension, Love without need, Truth without division. Oh, that I could see you, that I could behold you for a moment! But I know that I could not endure it, that my senses would not be able to bear the impression of the face of my heart's deepest longing. Created things wound me; human faces confound my sight. How could I then behold your glory?*

*Here in this desert, I perceive you better than before. By a great drama, you have "passed by" the world and shown yourself in a mode of revelation that at once is fully true and forthcoming but, at the same time, is gentle and humble so that the witness of it can heal us, even as it wrenches.*

*I perceive the Gospel now afresh: the babe in a manger; the teacher amid his friends; the innocent man suffering condemnation; the groom bereft and abandoned at the altar. You in your perfect rest are now submerged in our fruitless labor; you in your pure truth are tangled in our web of lies; you in*

*your ageless love are crying out in our abandonment and for-
sakenness; exhausted, broken, emptied and humiliated. Now
we can see you! You correspond with our senses, our sorrows,
our sinfulness, and our death. Now we can hear you speak,
and now we can answer your voice.*

*Yet you have done this all unchangingly. Your total trans-
formation into our time is but a revelation that you are always Love unmeasured, unbounded, unreserved. Your heart is
like the desert after all, and our hearts still retain enough of
your image to be able to find you as you are, in the condition
into which you came. You still bear the wounds in glory that
you showed after your Passion; the Lamb on the throne is still
the Lamb once slain.*

## The Monastic Mystique

JANUARY 28, WEDNESDAY

I spoke this morning to a seminarian who is newly consecrated, a priest in the diocese of Cairo who was just ordained by
Pope Shenouda. He will now make his forty-day retreat and receive his seminary education here at St. Bishoi Monastery during
that time.

He was pleasant and agreeable, but immediately he seemed
suspicious of what this American monk and anthropologist was
doing in the monastery. He feared that perhaps I was going to present the monastery in a superficial light, not necessarily even unfavorably, but in a way which could miss its genuine nature or its
more mysterious identity. He told me that only people who are
concerned with the inner life of faith should attempt to ponder the
history—or, what I think he meant, its sociological aspects—of a
monastery. Otherwise he is sure that one can never understand the
inner dynamism of a monastery and may inadvertently focus attention on its incidental aspects.

He told me that he thinks the monastery is not an institution
that somehow coasts on its own historical momentum. No matter
how long its history has been, he said, a monastery does not carry
on its life because it has a long heritage which keeps it afloat. If an
ancient monastery continues to keep its monks through time, it ex-

ists because an ageless faith remains the common life amongst its members. He said that, in reality, monasteries, despite all the fabulous protestations and appearances to the contrary, are creatures of the moment. That is, what they are *now*, they may not be at all in the future.

He reminded me that, of course, the desert is strewn with the ruins of monasteries that no longer exist. Those that remain and those that have long histories may be the ones that are more dramatic and the ones that catch our attention. They create the sense that there is a permanence about them. But the ones that no longer exist, the ones that have disintegrated, are the ones that should likewise teach us something important. Unless there is an ongoing life of faith and the mysterious impulse of grace, nothing abides, not even monasteries of great age and size and duration.

All things are provisional, this priest told me. The composition of a monastery and its discipline, its economy and its organization—all these things change, and are changeable, in relationship to the outside world around it. Even though the monasteries in the desert do not seem to respond to the changing outside world, he believes that the desert, especially, creates a raw kind of force which acts on the monastery. Though the monastery seems to be buffered and insulated by the desert, the fact is, he said, that the desert really subjects it to the effects of the Church's life and the life and the welfare of the people who live in the villages and the cities far away.

The great secret reality of the monastery is that it endures. Although it apparently repudiates the world far away, it nonetheless remains finely attuned to those aspects of the world of which it is the desert counterpoint. Were it not to do so, it would cease to draw vocations and would cease to have value for the Church. The way it becomes counterpoint to certain elements in the world is the way in which it addresses the heart of the Church, and the way in which the heart of the Church addresses the monastery.

If the monastery hasn't seemed to change, this young priest told me, it's because certain aspects of the world never change: human ambition, human selfishness, violence, and greed. These things remain common to all times and all places, to all secular peoples. These things remain the marks of their interrelations and their organizations and institutions. Monasteries seem to be changeless because they're always a counterpoint to these forces and to the institutions of the world. In some ways, monasteries can even tragically replicate certain aspects of these forces, even as a counterpoint can musically replicate the musical line to which it is contrasted. Nevertheless, the monastery attempts to be an iconographic contrast, and the desert makes it, in a certain sense, into a more brilliant reverse image. It gives it a higher profile, a louder microphone to address itself—not to the affairs of the public, but to the human heart and to the secret ear of the Church, wherever there are faithful Christians.

The young priest believes that there is a strong connection between the world and the desert, between the Church in the village and the monastery in the desert. He said there is a vital dialogue going on between them: a dialogue of signs, a dialogue of faith. He doesn't think that the desert (or the monastery in the desert, at least) can be cordoned off or separated from the dynamic life of the Church. It is a vital part—maybe even the heart—of the life of the Church. It captures the imagination of many who are on the edge of the Church, or outside it, and provides for them a genuine challenge to come to faith, to come into the presence of God.

### Coptic Etymology

JANUARY 29, THURSDAY

It was an overcast day and kind of windy, so I spent much of my afternoon in the library, looking through various books that are on reserve there, as well as speaking to the librarian, Abuna Tadros. As he was in an amiable mood and seemed more forthcoming than usual, I took advantage of the opportunity to ask him more about the monastery and about the Coptic Church.

I asked him about the etymology of the word *deir* by which they name a monastery. He told me that the word *deir* denotes people who are circling around a center, centered around a particular point. Abuna Tadros said, "A monastery is a place where monks are centered around their *kommos*, their spiritual father." In the Western Church, we would call him the "abbot" of the monastery.

For the Copts, the spiritual father provides a center—not around himself—but around God. The role of the *kommos* is to center the monastery around the Cross of our Lord Jesus in which the heart of God is revealed to us. It is to draw the monks into a more faithful observation of the Cross, a more faithful worship of the God who gave his love thereby, and a more careful patterning of their lives upon that model. The monastic life is, therefore, a spiritual-father or spiritual-direction-centered life, an obedience-centered life. It is a God-centered life, a Christ-centered life, and a Cross-centered life, all at once.

I asked Abuna Tadros about the eremitical life. Since a monastery is something which is centered, how is one to regard hermits, who live in isolation? He pointed out that all hermits are still Christ-centered, and that all monks remain centered around the Cross, centered around God. He said, "We are centered around the community of faith which makes God known to us by its charity, by our obedience to its authority, and by our perseverance in its ranks. It makes the Cross known to us by its friendships and by its tests. So the monk is still community-centered, even if he is living in a cave on a mountain, because he derived his faith from that community. He went through that community's formation process, and through the Holy Spirit he remains at prayer with and for that community."

I asked Abuna Tadros about the highest rank of the desert monk, the so-called *sowha*, the pilgrim monk who is absolutely cut off. The monks do not bring food to the mouth of the cave in which he lives, because he doesn't live in a cave. He roams about in the wilderness of the desert, living from the elements, the bare natural resources around him, having no fixed abode. Abuna Tadros said that such monks are the rarest and fewest of all.

He said that the *sowha* is really the exception. This monk is now closer to heaven than to earth, closer to the Communion of Saints, closer to the angels, closer to Christ Jesus risen than to the Church Militant which is still living in the midst of the world and struggling in the shadow of the Cross. Although this is such an exception, he said, the *sowha* still prays in the heart of the Church, and prays for the Church.

Incidentally, I cannot help but note that, while Abuna Tadros, speaking rather soberly, said that there are no *sowha* nearby, others have told me that there are. I think that Abuna Tadros is probably correct, that he is speaking realistically. The others, I suspect, say they are nearby because of the great lure of them. The stories about them and the fascination with them is so great that they have become a legend in the Church. They are always "nearby." Just as

*A Coptic Orthodox monk of the Wadi Natroun. He is wearing the qolunsha, a cap embroidered with crosses representing Christ and the Apostles.*

Abuna Tadros said, they are embedded in the heart of the Church. So the Church always envisions them, fashions them in her imagination as proximate, living, and vital, as contributing somehow to the present experience of the faithful.

The monastery has always had a way of embedding itself deeply in the imagination of the Church. There always should be *sowha*, from this point of view, who embody what that imagination suggests. But even if they are relatively few and far away, nevertheless, the romance about them and for them is great. If there can be such a great fascination with the *sowha* when they are far away, how much more powerful would it be if there were occasional examples of such monks available for the people of God to touch, to hear, and to see?

### The Baptism of the Desert

JANUARY 30, FRIDAY

I have not seen nor heard from Abuna Elia for quite a few days. I've heard only indirectly that he has either been ill, or is simply too cold to venture out of his cell. But this morning he sent for me, and after the Kodes I went to see him again in the courtyard of the garden next to his cell in the monastery. He was wearing a coat and a scarf, and looked a little worse for wear since the last time I saw him. He complained to me that this coldness is difficult to endure. I agreed with him that it is more difficult than the summer heat, and so we commiserated together a few moments. Then he had some things to discuss about which he had been praying and reading in the Scriptures.

The Copts, like Catholics, celebrate the Baptism of Jesus around the season of Christmas. They also read from the Gospels the various accounts of Jesus' baptism in the River Jordan by John. Abuna Elia explained to me that the baptism of Jesus was, in fact, two-fold. He said that Jesus was baptized, not only in the water of the Jordan, but also in the desert of Palestine. I asked him what he meant. He explained that the Gospels record that at the beginning of his public life, Jesus went down to the Jordan where John the Baptist was preaching and that he asked John to baptize him. John demurred, but Jesus prevailed, and John poured the water. When Jesus was coming up out of the water, the Gospels record that he heard a voice—perhaps others heard the voice as well: *"This is my beloved Son on whom my favor rests"* (Matthew 3:17).

Abuna Elia said that the baptism in the River Jordan was one of divine love and mercy, of divine affirmation. The Father's love was poured out upon the Son, and the Son enjoyed all that the Father gave him. But following the baptism in the Jordan, the Holy Spirit *drove* Jesus out into the desert. At least, so it is recorded by Mark in his Gospel when he says: "The Spirit *drove him out* into the desert" (Mark 1:12).

And here is the point Abuna Elia was making: that in the baptism of the Jordan, there is affirmation, but in the baptism of the desert there is temptation; there's a test. The baptism in the Jordan, the first of the two-fold baptism, is a baptism into divine life, a baptism into divine friendship, an immersion in the fullness of love. The baptism in the desert is a baptism into human alienation, into human estrangement from God. It is a dehydration, a hunger and thirst to which Christ Jesus freely gives himself for love of us. The first is the Father's act of love poured out upon Christ; the second is Christ's act of love poured out upon us. In both baptisms, the Holy Spirit figures very prominently, appearing in the form of a dove above Jesus in the Jordan for the first baptism and driving Jesus into the desert for the second.

In the same way that Jesus is driven by the Spirit of divine love and mercy into the desert, he is driven by that same Spirit to carry his Cross. He's compelled; he goes of an inner necessity, for the sake of love, for love of us. The second baptism of Jesus begins the process of a divine pursuit: the pursuit of human beings wherever we have fallen: into the lowest and the worst of places; into our greatest suffering, our greatest despair and our deepest sin; even unto death.

In reality, said Abuna Elia, the work of the Spirit began in the womb of the Virgin Mary, the place where he was first conceived. The womb of the Virgin Mary was like the baptism in the Jordan. Just as the Holy Spirit hovered over the waters of creation, so the Holy Spirit hovered over the Virgin Mary when Christ Jesus was conceived in her (Luke 1:35). The womb is a watery place into which we are all received; it is a place of affirmation, a place where we are conceived in love. Certainly, Christ Jesus was conceived in love.

But it was also like the baptism in the desert because, paradoxically, the womb into which Christ Jesus was conceived was deeply troubled. According to St. Luke, from the moment in which the archangel greeted Mary, she was viscerally, physically, wrenched (cf. Luke 1:29). And so Christ Jesus began his descent into the troubled waters of our humanity from the moment of his conception. Indeed, Mary's participation in this mystery was not incidental.

Simeon reinforced the same idea, suggesting that the rejection of the Word made flesh would result in the piercing of Mary's heart as well (Luke 2:35). From the beginning, when Christ was conceived in Mary's womb, then in his infancy when Jesus was presented in the temple, and finally, as she stood beneath the Cross, Mary participated in the suffering of her Son. But her Son's suffering is our suffering. She is the mother of all who suffer.

Abuna Elia said, "In Mary, Christ Jesus began his descent into our humanity, into our suffering, so it is also in her that we begin our ascent to his love. Our sufferings have become the place of his visitation ever since she accepted his coming into her troubled heart, into her womb. Our desert becomes a watered garden by his visit. There is, in the desert of our suffering, a secret fountain, the hidden spring of her prayer, just as in the desert of the Wadi Natroun, the ancient subterranean rivers of the Nile are still providing water these thousands of years later.

"A moral point to all of this," said Abuna Elia, "is that we must accept the pattern of the great commute in our life. We must enjoy the feast of divine affirmation when it is presented, most especially in the Eucharist. On every occasion of grace and mercy, we must enjoy the blessing. But at the same time, we must be willing to be driven by the Spirit into the desert, into the work that we must do for others in compassion. We must go out into the desert of our own purification and sanctification. We must accept the eventualities of Divine Providence which come to us with the same Spirit of affirmation who came over Jesus in the waters of the Jordan, the Spirit who likewise drove him into the desert where he was alone and abandoned, the Spirit who drove him even to the Cross. We do these things in union with Christ Jesus in the prayer of Mary, for it was by her prayer, her *Fiat*, that this process was initiated. God came to visit us to make this fountain of life flow into our desert."

I reflected afterwards about what Abuna Elia had shared with me, comparing it to my own experience of these few months in the desert and to my own earlier reflections on the Baptism of Jesus and his subsequent wilderness sojourn. It seems to me that what Abuna Elia said is an appropriate measure of the ambivalence of the desert, for it is certainly a hostile environment. It is one which impoverishes its inhabitants and intimidates anyone who passes through it. Yet, at the same time, if one is patient and does not rush through it too quickly, he can discover its hidden springs. There is a kind of silence, for instance, in which the word of God can echo and be better heard in his heart. There is a peace in the desert that relativizes all the stresses and troubles of human life in the city. The desert baptizes us into the worst of our human weakness, but it transforms that weakness into genuine poverty before God. Rather than a place that fosters our pretenses and illusions about ourselves, it is a means by which we are baptized into the truth of divine love, divine life.

I remember the closing words of the Latin Mass: *"Ite, missa est* —Go, get out!"* which we try to soften in the English translation as "Go in peace." But the Mass is a dismissal: *missa, dismissa.* We are sent away; we are shown out. We are driven by the Spirit of affirmation we have enjoyed in the Mass to go out into the desert of the world around us to be emissaries of Christ, occasions of blessing. We are to draw the springs up from the desert in which we walk, so that, wherever our steps take us, the secret running rivers of divine friendship and grace will flow. What does the Psalmist say? *They walk through the barren desert and they make it a place of flowing springs* (cf. Psalm 84:7).

## *Of Paul and John*

JANUARY 31, SATURDAY

My discussion today with Abuna Elia considered the relationship of St. Paul and St. John and their messages. For St. Paul, Abuna Elia said, the whole purpose and work of Christ Jesus is summed up in his Cross. He preaches Christ and Christ crucified; he preaches the Cross of our Lord Jesus. He doesn't preach any particular miracle of Jesus or any particular message of Jesus. Rather, he continually sums up the mission of Jesus by his death and Resurrection. This is fitting, after all, Abuna Elia said, because Paul didn't know Jesus in Galilee; he didn't participate in the earthly ministry of Jesus. He met Jesus in the Resurrection on the road to Damascus, and in that meeting he was persuaded of his life, his message, and his lordship. So this is the message he continually reinforces: a summation of Christ in his Paschal work.

St. Paul calls the Paschal work of Jesus "God's secret plan," hidden through all ages, but now revealed in Christ. He calls it "a hidden wisdom or mystery," the meaning of which is now made clear in the suffering of Jesus and his glory. Abuna Elia said, "For Paul, the self-emptying work of Christ Jesus, his suffering, his kenotic work is, in fact, our rest. It is the work of God in which we rest. It is the life of grace anticipated by the Sabbath rest in the Old Testament. This grace elicits from us the act of faith by which we rest in the Paschal work of Christ."

This was a good summation of St. Paul, I thought, and Abuna Elia tied it nicely to St. John. He said it was natural for John to adopt the insight of Paul and develop it further, seeing in the age-old plan of the Paschal Mystery revealed in Christ a revelation of a timeless pattern in God himself. God would not reveal something that was incongruent with himself. Since Christ Jesus is his highest revelation, we have the right to believe that it is a revelation that was intentional, a revelation of God himself. This age-old plan of God is a laying bare of a pattern of love in God. The Word, the Logos, was made flesh. For John, the secret wisdom of the Father, this Word which was learned in eternity, the Son obeyed and imitated. The mysterious wisdom of the Father was a self-emptying love, so there's a relationship between the Father and the Son, a similarity in imitation. What the Son was learning through all eternity, he came as man to teach us from the Cross.

So it makes great sense, then, that in the Book of Revelation the Lamb of God who was slain not only bears forever the marks of his slaughter; he is also the Lamb who was slain from the foundation of the world. Long before the Paschal Mystery was actually accomplished on the Mount of Calvary, the Paschal Mystery was enfolded into the Trinity and ascribed to the Person of the Son who learned this from his Father.

I think that Abuna Elia has been profoundly engaged with the Paschal Mysteries in his own life as a desert monk. He has had occasion to contemplate them both in terms of his own journey in solitude and in terms of the suffering of his people. For him, the Paschal Mysteries are vivid. They are realized in us, and our realization of them gives us insight into their original meaning in Christ. It is from this vantage point that Abuna Elia is able to gain extraordinary insights. He also reads a variety of patristic and theological sources from a wide background, which he is able to integrate into his prayer life and into the insights which he shares with me.

# FEBRUARY
## A TIME TO INTERCEDE

## *Of Apparitions and Miracles*

FEBRUARY 1 AND 2, SUNDAY AND MONDAY

There were many pilgrims in the monastery today. Some of them alerted the abbot to a phenomenon occurring in Cairo—one that I think he was already familiar with. They reminded him that there have been apparitions of the Virgin Mary in a church called Sitt Damiana, the Church of the Lady Damiana. Anba Serabamon realized, having just seen me before the pilgrims spoke to him, that I had not visited this church in Cairo, and he regarded my pilgrimage to Egypt as being incomplete until or unless I went there to ask for the Virgin Mary's favor. So I agreed to accompany the pilgrims when they returned to Cairo today.

The abbot recommended that I go to the church later in the evening so there would be fewer people visiting and I would not be besieged. Desert monks, especially at shrine sites like this, are always being asked for blessings and special prayers by the crowds. So I went back to Cairo with the pilgrims and waited a while in their flat, which is not far from this church in Shubra. At nearly 11:00 P.M., they took me to the church.

The pastor of the church let me in; I was given a place to pray in the otherwise empty and darkened building. After a few minutes, the door of the church opened and a group of children came in. They were the nieces and nephews of the priest who had let me in. Because they lived nearby, he got them up so that they could receive a blessing from the monk who lives in the desert. I explained to the children that I am really an American monk and that I am just visiting the desert. They could hardly understand me, and they didn't care. It was late at night and they wanted a blessing. (In Egypt, to give a blessing, one says a prayer while putting a wooden hand-cross on the person's head. The monks had given me one to carry in my pocket when I arrived at the monastery.)

So I blessed the children with the hand-cross and they went away. Five minutes later they came back with their friends: fifteen of them now, and *they* wanted a blessing. When these children left, they came back with their parents and their uncles and their aunts. By midnight the church was filled! Even at that hour, they turned out to receive a blessing, such is the lively faith in this district near the church. They were coming up the aisle toward me like a solid Communion line. So there I was, putting the wooden cross on peoples' heads, giving each of them a blessing.

While I was thus occupied, those who had already received a blessing went out the back of the church into an open-air court-yard. Soon they began to shout, *"Shuf, el Adra! Halwah alwee!* Look! the Virgin! How sweet she is!" and to point to the air above the church. They could see the Virgin Mary there! I didn't know it then, but that was, in fact, where she most often appeared: outside, above the church. But I was under the roof on the inside and I didn't see anything. I expected that everyone, the whole mob, would all rush out to see the apparition. But they didn't. They stayed right where they were. They had come for a blessing and they were going to get it, no matter what! It occurred to me that the apparitions were well known to the inhabitants of the district round about. My eagerness to see them was not the same as theirs. I tried to push my way through the crowd to get to the back of the church. Actually, I had to try to make an opening by blessing people to my right and to my left to get through.

I had almost reached a place where I thought I would be able to see what the people outside were seeing when suddenly, in front of me, stood a little man in a brown suit. He couldn't have been more than five feet tall. He was carrying a small bundle. He had a very sad look on his face; his eyes were sunken in. He had been crying—and not just for a day or two. His expression was that of someone who has known grief for a long time. He put his little bundle in my arms and explained to me, in English, that he is a doctor, that his wife had died in childbirth, and that this baby, his daughter, was a month old.

She didn't look any older than a week or two. He had taken her to many specialists and they had given up all hope. She could die at any moment. Actually, the baby looked more dead than alive. He told me that she had never opened her eyes or moved her limbs or cried since she was born. She hadn't grown at all. It was all they could do to force nutrition down her throat. Could I give his baby a blessing?

Well, I froze on the spot. It was a very awkward situation. I had people in front of me pointing to the heavens and shouting that they could see the Virgin Mary. I had people behind me pressing to get a blessing. I had a man, a widower, crumpled in front of me, and I had his dying baby in my arms. It was not something for which I had been trained in the seminary, and I really didn't know what to do. I was standing near the open doorway. The wind, which had been picking up, was whipping through the congregation, so I laid the cloth scapular of my habit over the baby to protect her from the bitter cold. To hold it down, I placed my wooden hand-cross on top of the scapular to keep it intact on the baby.

That's all I did, and I did it in a kind of automatic fashion, spontaneously, just as a means of keeping the baby warm, not knowing what else I could do. But apparently the father of the child thought that this was some kind of special blessing, hiding the baby under the scapular with my cross on top. He got down on his knees and everyone else in the church, now watching us, quieted, and got down on their knees too. The whole congregation was praying, but I was standing there, frozen. I don't remember praying; God forgive me. I don't remember saying a blessing, or even thinking a blessing. I only remember being paralyzed.

In a few minutes the people who were shouting outside stopped shouting because the apparition had passed—an apparition I never got to see, although I had come here for that purpose. When the people outside grew quiet, everybody inside the church got up. I removed the scapular and the cross from the baby and gave her back to her father. And there in her father's arms the baby opened her eyes. She took a deep gulp of air and let out a cry! She began to move her arms, and her complexion, which had been brown and gray, turned pink in a moment! The little man began crying and laughing at the same time and the people in the congregation, who quickly learned what had happened, became jubilant with gratitude and praise. Arabic ululations (their tongue-rolling sound of joy) filled the church!

Just then some of the people who had seen the apparition came into the church and said, "Abuna, why didn't you come outside to see the miracle?" The father of the baby said, "We didn't have to go outside to see a miracle. Through the Virgin above us, God gave us a miracle right here by blessing my baby!" The people went home and brought back picnic baskets of fruits and breads and sat on the floor of the church and celebrated until dawn.

These people are a people of faith. They know how to be touched by God. I felt that I was little more than a prop in that church—a prop that held a baby and kept the wind from making her cold. But the faith of these people was open to the grace of God. Because they were able to see beyond me to God, they were able to receive this marvelous gift from him. They know how to be Church; they know how to admire even unworthy earthen vessels, how to be open to blessings from God through such vessels. Their faith, their openness, was all that counted. It was their faith, their prayers, that brought that baby back to health by the grace of God.

I asked the father of the baby for his name and address and told him that I would like to meet him again when I next came back to Cairo, to see how he and the child were doing. He gladly provided this information for me, and I departed from this festive place to retire to my friends' house in Cairo from which I would be safely taken back to the monastery soon thereafter.


FEBRUARY 4, WEDNESDAY

I've been spending the last few days at the home of Mr. Kamal-Hanna, his wife, Juliet, and their son Emil. I've been speaking to them about my experience at Sitt Damiana. They are completely at ease with the story, because events such as these are part of their daily conversation. However, they acknowledged this occurrence to be rather extraordinary, even in Coptic Egypt, where miracles abound. The sharing of such stories with one another is their delight, and it reinforces their faith. Some years earlier, this family saw the apparitions of the Virgin Mary at the Church of Our Lady of the Olives at Zeitoun. They saw her in an extraordinary way there. She appeared in the form of a radiant figure, also in the air above the church, like the apparitions at Sitt Damiana. They described the event in detail and how they were touched and moved by it. They told me how the crowd responded, and how completely given over they were to the blessing, the grace of the night. The Coptic people of Egypt are particularly receptive and open to blessings such as these. What a contrast to the apathy of many Churches in the West in which people don't really seem to be so open or excited to be blessed by God! Perhaps they are not so aware of their need.

## February 5, Thursday

I made my way back to the Patriarchate this morning and waited near the cathedral steps till the entourage left for the desert. The Pope returns to St. Bishoi Monastery for his weekend retreat every Thursday, and I get to travel back with him, or at least in one of the cars, as in this case.

Traveling from the city to the desert is ordinarily jarring. The clutter and the pressures of Cairo are extreme. The desert itself is an extreme in the opposite direction: emptiness and silence. But traveling from the Church in the city to the Church in the desert is not nearly so jarring. The faith of the people in Cairo and the faith of the monks in the desert is the same faith. Both the Copts in the city and the Copts in the desert are filled with the same Spirit and the same blessing, so there's naturally much more dialogue between the city and the desert for those who belong to the same Church.

## February 8, Sunday

> *O Lord of Light,*
>
> *You who made the stars, how blinding is the sun to my eyes! Even in these "wintry" days when it arcs lower across the sky, it illuminates the sand with uncompromised brilliance. In summer, you made its rays stronger and more direct, but now in winter you have hung it so low that it is no longer reflected in my field of vision but, of itself, it peers into my sight. How commanding it is; how provocative and assertive to my senses.*
>
> *And how wrong it is that men have ever mistaken creatures for you, my Creator. But if they have erred thus, how right that only the greatest creature should have sufficed for the confusion.*

*The children of the Pharaohs worshiped the sun in igno-rance, but may it have been that beneath the clouds of their misunderstanding was the light of true aspiration for you, whom we have even called "Sun of Justice"? May the affects of our bodies and the yearning of our senses seek you with greater zeal than the ramblings of our minds. May we by our hearts and wills receive the grace, the light and warmth of your Pres-ence when our reason cannot comprehend the transparent sim-plicity of your truth. "Let there be light" were your first words in the created world. They also express the deepest aspiration of created souls who have too long dwelt in the shadows.*

*I plead for all right-minded men, Merciful God, who, by their merely intellectual assent to the truths you have re-vealed, grow self-assured of the system of thought they profess and forget you, Truth itself, upon whom they are always de-pendent. Then the "light" they see shrouds them in darkness, and your sun does not shine upon them. May I not be one of them, and may they not remain there. Let the sun of your justice shine upon us; or, rather, let the "Morning Star" of your mercy be our true light.*

*This desert sun commands all sight and rules the day in its might, regardless of the season of the year or the angle of its rays. May it reflect your Presence to us in every creature at every moment and in every sense, till we have grown old in your friendship. May we even see you refracted through the density of pain and weariness in the faces of those whose look burdens us with our darkest feelings.*

*Rather, help me to be like these sun-drenched grandchildren of the Pharaohs who first reflected your light to me, and through whom I can now see your light refracted, your face revealed.*

### From the Navy to the Altar

FEBRUARY 10, TUESDAY

I interviewed a priest from the Diocese of Cairo today. Al-though he is more than fifty-five years of age, he's only recently been ordained and is now practicing the rituals of the Coptic Church in this monastery. His congregation recommended him for Holy Orders, voted for him, in fact, so that Pope Shenouda received and ordained him for that diocese, to serve the parish from which he comes.

He was once a naval officer. He told me that he had fought in three wars in the service of the Egyptian navy and was never once afraid. But now, before the altar, he said, he is always trembling. He is a good example of Coptic spirituality, because he recognizes that to approach the altar is to approach the living God. This lays bare all that is fragile and delicate and vulnerable in us. It also exposes all that is sinful in us, either to judgment or to mercy, depending upon our honesty and our humility before God.

## Gifts of the Spirit

FEBRUARY 12, THURSDAY

Abuna Elia told me today that there are, ideally, an indefinite number of positions or niches to be occupied, if the Church is to have its fullest orchestration, if the Church is to be fully functional in the world. For, he said, the Church is a great parade which can be displayed in its entirety only if all of its segments are fully engaged in any given age or generation. The Body of Christ can fulfill its mission upon the earth to touch, to heal, to speak only when there are sufficient numbers of people to perform its various ministries.

That is the work of the Holy Spirit, Abuna Elia said, to constitute the Body of Christ by providing various members with his various gifts. He quoted from St. Paul's Letter to the Corinthians that to some it was given to be apostles, prophets, teachers, or healers (cf. 1 Corinthians 12:6-10). But he also said that this is not merely a functional unity of so many interactive parts. Rather, it is a mosaic, or an iconographic unity, where Christ is witnessed not only to the world outside the Church but also to the various members within its own life. The Church has a "visual, apostolic mission" to fulfill and to uphold.

He reminded me of Christ Jesus on the mountain as a backdrop to his historical life and public mission. Christ on the mountain was not just preparing and praying for that mission. We are told that, sometimes, he went there to remain true to his mission. There is one story in the Gospels in which, after Christ had fed the five thousand, he was aware that the crowd intended to crown him king, so he fled from them to the mountain to pray alone.

Abuna Elia said that the people were going to falsify Christ's mission. They were going to tempt him to self-exaltation and self-fulfillment, to turn him against the godly work of self-emptying. Christ fled from this temptation so that he could continue his mission, both in terms of his dialogue with the Father and in terms of his Passion. When Peter attempted to dissuade Christ from his sacrificial work of the Cross, Jesus disassociated himself even from his friend and vicar: *"Get behind me, you Satan!"* (Matthew 16:23). At his critical moment of self-emptying, Christ Jesus would be alone, even forsaken.

So the monk is called to the mountain or to the desert to pray alone and, when in community, to pray from a lonely interiority. He prays for the Church and for his own particular mission when it is given to him. But he also summons the Church to greater authenticity, to be a sign to priests, to Religious, to the clergy, to the laity: a sign of self-emptying love, self-emptying dedication to God's will. He prays to be a sign which summons the Church to genuine faith and poverty of spirit before the world.

Ultimately, Abuna Elia said, even though the monk is isolated and apparently far away from the heart of all the Church's activity, if he is faithful, the Church will fashion herself around him and reconstitute Christ's body with him. Such being the case, the Church will always be able to inspire martyrs. This is all to the good because, in the case of the Coptic Church, a lack of readiness to raise up martyrs would, in fact, be a sign or even a cause of the Church's overall decline. No matter how apparently disorganized and oppressed the institution of the Coptic Church may have seemed, its spirit has always been prepared to instill such a degree of holiness among its members that there were those in every age willing to suffer and to die that they might bear witness to the mission of Christ in the world.

### Forty Days

FEBRUARY 15, SUNDAY

The monastery here involves itself more and more deeply in its preparations for Lent. Just as in the Western Church, Lent is a period of about seven weeks' duration which, except for Sundays, is therefore a forty-day period of preparation for Easter.

But in the Coptic Church, there are some undertones to the Lenten season that I had not realized before. I never knew there was a Nilotic link to Lent. The monks tell me that, historically, the time from the cresting of the floodwater of the Nile to the time when it returned to its banks was a period of forty days. After the flood, the people of Egypt had to wait on the edges of the Nile Valley forty days more before they could return to their fields, their villages, their homes.

When they finally returned, a fresh layer of mud overlaid everything. A great deal of work was required to remove it from their homes. But they were forbidden to complain about it, because that mud was the source of all life in Egypt. All the fecundity of the fields, all the bounty of the harvest derived from that mud. So they would wait patiently and gratefully for the flood to pass before they could return home to a new and fertile world.

This was the background of the children of Israel who had lived in Egypt for centuries. So when they passed through the "flood" waters of the Red Sea and then "waited" forty years before they could enter into the Promised Land, they had already been prepared in Egypt for a period of waiting. They expected to wait an interval of time marked by the number "forty" before they could come home to the place which was fertile, which was rich with "milk and honey," and rich with the blessings and the bounty of God. Like the Egyptians, the Hebrews were also enjoined not to complain about the hardships which had to be borne if they were to enter the Promised Land. Such complaining, as described in the Book of Exodus, is the intended reference in St. Benedict's *Rule* against "murmuring." Much of what people complain about is often, paradoxically, an occasion of some future blessing.

Abuna Elia also told me that, of course, forty weeks also comprises the gestation period, the period of nine solar months in which a child is formed in the womb before being born into the world. Such a period of time prepares the unborn to grow, to become large enough and strong enough to survive in the outside world. The baby must go through the watery abyss of the maternal womb before coming home to the common air which we all breathe.

In other words, the period of time marked by the interval of "forty" is inscribed in the Copts' personal histories, in their public life, in their national history, in their liturgical life, and in divine revelation. It is, therefore, a period of time which is also calibrated for worship. It is a time of preparation to pass through the waters of baptism into the Promised Land of intimacy and union with

God. For all Christians, it is no less a time to renew that process by repentance and prayer. Enough of murmuring complaints, therefore. Let us "enter in," and receive the blessing!

### Of Sand Boxes and Prayer Petitions

FEBRUARY 17, TUESDAY

In the church of this monastery, just as in all the Coptic churches throughout Egypt, there is, of all things, a sand box! Of course, the Copts don't think of it so much as a sand box but as a candle stand. They light their prayer candles and embed them in the sand with their prayer intentions in order that the candles may remain afire in the church as a sign of those petitions long after those who lit the candles have gone. While the Copts are especially mindful of the candle and its prayerful flame, I am just as much fascinated by the sand itself.

The sand of the desert is all around us. It surrounds this monastery. The sand box forms a miniature desert within the monastery church: an "inner desert," as it were. The desert outside holds the monks within the realm of prayer; the desert within holds up their candles of prayer to the face of God. So, following the local convention, I trace the names of the people for whom I pray in the sand of the candle stand, and then set a candle in the traces of their names.

Abuna Elia once told me to trace the prayer intentions about which I feel most deeply into the desert floor itself. Later he sent me back to find the place where I had written them. "Was there any answer there?"

"No," I answered, "I couldn't even find the spot; the desert wind had covered over every trace of the petitions I had inscribed in the sand."

"That is your answer," he replied. He meant that, as the sands had covered the traces of the prayer, so my petitions themselves should yield to grace, that I need not revisit needs which have been entrusted to Providence. Trust, he said, is better even than perseverance in prayer, and perseverance, so far as the petitionary aspect of prayer is concerned, has its value in slowly evoking greater trust. Otherwise, it would not be wise to describe such an exercise as "perseverance in prayer," but rather, "subjection to worry."

*A Coptic monk on the roof of the Monastery of the Romans.*

FEBRUARY 18, WEDNESDAY

*Divine Redeemer,*

*Forgive me, Lord; I had not listened and I did not trust you. You had said that your chosen people were to be a "blessing" to all nations, and that your disciples would be a "leaven" in the dough of the world. But somehow I had imagined that the success of your Providence could be measured only when all nations were baptized into your Church. And I still acknowledge that the mission of our faith will perdure till there is a universal inclusion of all humanity in the Communion of Christ. But I also yield to the truth you revealed that the success of our mission lies in the witness we bear, even to those we cannot visibly include in our closest fellowship. The witness we bear, if we bear it lovingly, peaceably, and with respect for all persons, is the "blessing" you promised to Abraham and to his descendants. The service we render, even to those who cannot imitate us or be grateful to us, is the "leaven" that mysteriously makes the dough of our heavily laden culture rise into a civilization of justice.*

*I need not fret that your people have always failed to promote your kingdom, Lord. I need not survey the wreckage of sacred history which groans at our folly. You were succeeding in the midst of people even such as these! And even when all our failures came together, and rejection and refusal, abandonment and forsakenness were the response the world gave to you because of us, yet you had the power to make these failures your greatest sign of Providence in the Cross.*

*You have compelled me, Lord, to reassess these people, your "holy family" of Coptic Christians, whom Christendom neglects and regards as failures. They have not, after all, baptized the nation and converted the Moslems. Their numbers, even as they increase, are an ever smaller part of the whole population. But I marvel now how all Egyptians regard them. Even grudgingly and judgmentally, they cannot fail to find some sign of your Presence in them and your kindness toward them. Now I see how, in their seeming insignificance, they serve the Moslems by their presence, bearing witness to you in fairness, honesty, gentleness, and kindness.*

> *Even more wonderfully, Good God, I observe the monks themselves who are somehow a leaven in the dough of their Church, the heart of the heart of your kingdom here. I praise you for them, who summon their people, and even me, to rise up to the challenge of your Covenant.*

## A Visitor from the States

FEBRUARY 20, FRIDAY

Father James Bump, a friend of mine for many years, has come to visit! He arrived in the monastery late this morning, having been offered a driver by my associates in Cairo. However, I noticed that the driver was told to wait for us. So, a few hours later, after I had given Father Jim a tour of the monastery, he announced that I would be going back to Cairo as his guest in the city, that we would not be staying here in the monastery! I think that he was impressed positively by the austerity of the monastery and its rustic simplicity, but decided that it was not his vocation to visit it at length. So with good spirits and good humor, we returned to Cairo in the evening. How exquisite are Near Eastern monastic schedules; from day to day and moment to moment, everything can change!

FEBRUARY 21, SATURDAY

We visited a number of my friends in Cairo and made arrangements for a more protracted tour of the country in the next few days, as well as a brief tour of Israel thereafter.

## Good News!

FEBRUARY 23, MONDAY

Some very good news! Today I was able to go to Bank Misr and recover the funds which I had originally wired to this bank when I first left the States in September. For all these months I have been traveling virtually without any money, although there has been no particular liability about this when living in the monastery.

However, now that I have left the monastery for a few days of touring, it's a great advantage to be able to draw from these resources. I had some of my new friends in Cairo ask their business associates to search various Bank Misrs until the funds I had wired could be located. A few days ago I received a tip about where they had been deposited, so I was able to retrieve the money today. Now I shall be able to travel appropriately in the company of my friend and pay my own expenses. But it was marvelous in a certain way not to have had any money at all for all these months, to have simply experienced the charity and the hospitality of the desert monks. God has been taking very good care of me.

## Historic Sites

### FEBRUARY 25, WEDNESDAY

Well, we have had almost a week of touring. We've seen the traditional sights in Karnac and Luxor and Aswan. We've taken a *feluca*, a boat ride across the Nile, and visited Elephantine Island in Upper Egypt—a site which is very interesting archaeologically.

It seems that there was a sizable Jewish community on that island for several centuries. They may have even had a genuine temple—oddly, a temple with sacrificial holocausts and offerings, parallel to the temple in Jerusalem. One wonders why a Jewish settlement would have temple sacrifice outside of Jerusalem long after David consolidated Hebrew worship in his own city. This unusual Nilotic temple ruin and the monasteries of the Ethiopian wilderness are giving me the idea that I should title my anthropological ethnography "Sacrifice in the Desert." I recall from the Book of Exodus that Moses was commissioned by God to offer sacrificial worship in the desert after he led Israel forth out of Egypt. At any rate, we saw a great deal of Egypt and visited some of the various Christian churches as well as Muslim mosques.

## Pope Shenouda's Audience

I took Father Jim to Pope Shenouda's Wednesday evening audience tonight where five thousand people were in attendance— mostly young people. As noted before, the Pope's whole format is simply to take questions from a question box and to answer them at some length for nearly two hours. The congregation listened with almost bated breath and responded with fairly wild applause as the Pope gave very traditional answers to the difficult questions which were being raised.

I continue to find it remarkable that the straightforward, firm, theological, and pastoral approach of this Pope elicits such enthusiastic and joyful response from the youth of his Church. I can only note the dramatic difference between Pope Shenouda's responses to the young and the manner by which we attempt to attract our own youth into the life of the Church in the West. To win them, we sometimes water down and soften the clear outlines of our faith and its pastoral applications. Father Jim and I were very impressed, not only by the zeal of the Coptic Pope, but most especially by the Coptic youth who attended as they evidenced their profound sense of faith and commitment to the traditions of their Church.

And, of course, as usual, the young people surrounded us afterwards, asking all kinds of questions about why we are in Egypt and about our faith and our prayer life. So we stayed up till quite late talking to them there in the plaza of the cathedral, and enjoyed ourselves immensely in the midst of that profoundly committed faith community. "Just like our young people's reaction to church services in America!" Father Jim sadly joked.

### The Bible of the Nile

FEBRUARY 26, THURSDAY

Today we traveled south of Cairo to visit St. Mary's Church in Maadi, which is located directly on the Nile itself. This church is regarded by the Copts as marking the place where the Holy Family embarked from this region to travel by boat to Upper Egypt. So it is a holy site for the Copts, this place visited by Jesus, Mary, and Joseph; it is a site of special veneration for them.

Some years ago, a Bible was found floating on the Nile River nearby. It was opened to the passage of the prophet Isaiah which speaks about Egypt as one day being a place from which true worship of God would rise up:

> *On that day there shall be an altar to the LORD in the land of Egypt, and a sacred pillar to the LORD near the boundary. It*

*shall be a sign and a witness to the Lord of hosts in the land of Egypt, when they cry out to the LORD against their oppressors, and he sends them a savior to defend and deliver them. The LORD shall make himself known to Egypt, and the Egyptians shall know the LORD in that day; they shall offer sacrifices and oblations, and fulfill the vows they make to the LORD. Although the LORD shall smite Egypt severely, he shall heal them; they shall turn to the LORD and he shall be won over and heal them. (Isaiah 19:19-22)*

And so the Copts look to this site as a providential sign for them that one day, because of their presence in Egypt, the whole nation will be especially blessed to worship God in spirit and in truth. That "floating Bible" is still on display in the church.

It is a compelling sight to see the Copts here, because when they visit the site and see that Bible, they are deeply moved. I suppose it brings together a variety of themes for them. Jesus, Mary, and Joseph were here, of course; the whole idea of their being in flight as "the first Palestinian refugees," the Copts say, fleeing their persecutors, is something poignant for them, especially since, living in Egypt, they are also a people suffering a certain degree of marginalization.

The water of the Nile saturates the whole setting. Since the Bible which was found there was soaked in the Nile, the Nile fills the whole scene with its power. Or, rather, it may be said that the Word of God soaks the Nile with its power, and that the Word of God gives to this scene a transforming, transfiguring power, turning persecution and flight into an opportunity of grace, an occasion or summons for worship, a call to the nation for conversion.

There are two overlapping images here: Jesus, Mary, and Joseph on a bark floating down the Nile: the Word made flesh in the midst of the Nile. And the other view: that of the written Word, the printed Word, the biblical Word likewise floating down the Nile in its own case, in its own cover. For the Copts, these two images, overlapping each other, coinciding with each other, mutually inter-associated with each other, are very enriching. For the Coptic people really do enjoy the Scriptures in exactly that way. The Word of God has such an energy for them that it continually radiates outward from itself and permeates their whole experience. It saturates their difficulties, their crosses, and their problems as well as their prayers and their joys with its transforming power.

## Prayers for the Afflicted

FEBRUARY 27, FRIDAY

Today we visited St. George Monastery for nuns in Old Cairo. It is in an almost subterranean section of the city, below the present surface of the city by several meters. There is a room in the basement of this monastery with a large chain affixed to the wall. From time to time rather severely troubled people are brought in to be chained to the wall here. They spend some hours or a night in chains, while the Sisters above pray that St. George may visit them and bring liberation from whatever evil is besetting them.

Some of the Westerners in our group thought this was a terribly disturbing and psychologically oppressive practice. But I find it altogether a consoling thought to be the object of the prayers of the sisters above and the solicitude of the saint below in order to be freed by just a few hours of wrenching transition rather than spend months or years of one's life in an in-between state of mental disability.

It is precisely because the Coptic people have such cultural unity and religious and spiritual consensus that they can avail themselves of the grace of such experiences as these. It is precisely because we in the West lack such a consensus and are deprived of such a spiritual understanding of the world around us that we cannot make use of such cathartic rites. Instead, we assume that such practices have to do with superstition or ignorance. I am not so sure at all that this is superstition or ignorance. I wonder, indeed, if the Copts might not have a significantly higher rate of success in caring for their troubled and disturbed members than do we— with all of our much more refined apparatus of purely secular psychology. Grace builds on nature and must also build on culture as well, which is, after all, "connatural" to man. After all, we do grapple with realities "seen and unseen," whether we realize it or not. Why not seek the assistance of a saint who shares in the ministry of the Cross to combat the darkness and the evils around us?

FEBRUARY 28, SATURDAY

This morning, Father Jim and I went to the government building, the *mugamma*, to purchase our visas so that we could make a brief trip to Israel. It would be my first and his second visit to Israel, and going there is part of his pilgrimage. It is difficult to get a visa; the bureaucracy of Egypt is very tedious. We spent hours going from desk to desk to get various stamps. But finally we purchased our bus tickets and got our visas. These two nations were at war not so long ago; travel and commerce between them is by no means simple!

# MARCH
## A TIME TO GO ON PILGRIMAGE

### *On to Israel*

MARCH 1, SUNDAY

We rose at 4:15 A.M. and waited outside the Heliopolis Sheraton for our bus. After a long ride from Cairo to Port Said to cross the Suez Canal, we then made our way through Sinai, clearing customs. At the border of Egypt and Israel we had to change buses, for no bus is permitted to make the entire passage. The Egyptian bus stops at the border and lets the passengers out. They then board an Israeli bus.

We finally arrived in Jerusalem late in the afternoon and were taken to the monastery Ecce Homo along the Via Dolorosa where we found rooms at fifteen dollars a night, including breakfast. Not a bad deal, indeed! We concelebrated Mass this evening in their chapel and enjoyed a 7:00 supper with a Parisian priest who knows some of our confreres back at St. Vincent. After dinner we regaled a group of visiting Sisters plus another priest and a lay woman with tales of the Egyptian desert and the Coptic Church. This is, of course, the kind of repartee that pilgrims in the Holy Land or anywhere else always share: stories of the road.

### *A Tour of the Old City*

MARCH 2, MONDAY

After breakfast, a certain Sister Mary Mark, whose brother had translated into English the biography of Anna Catherine Emmerich, the German mystic and stigmatist, gave us a tour of the Old City. We walked along the Via Dolorosa to the site of the Passion and the Holy Sepulcher. We visited the Coptic Ethiopians in Deir Sultan, the monastery claimed by the Egyptian Copts as well. Indeed, the network of chapels, grottos, caves, altars, and ambulatories at this site are claimed by six different rites and Churches!

Along our tour, we stopped at the Dormition, a Benedictine abbey, and were treated to hot chocolate in its cafe. It has been a cold and drizzly day here in Jerusalem. Sister Mary Mark walked us through the Jewish Quarter and then through the Carga, an old Byzantine shopping district in that section of the city. Nearby we saw King David's tomb and the Cenacle. We breezed by the Dome of the Rock Mosque to the so-called "Wailing Wall," where I inserted several prayer requests on folded papers for a number of Copts who insisted that I take their prayers to the holy city and ask God's blessing for them.

Then we returned to Ecce Homo and Father Jim and I passed through the Lion's Gate out of the walled city, but not before we had photographed the Golden Gate where the Messiah is supposed to return in glory one day. Once out of the city, we climbed up the hillside of the Kedron which was very steep and slippery today. At the top, we failed to gain entry into the Church of the Ascension because it was locked. However, we did find our way into the Chapel of the Ascension which displays a stone with the alleged "footprint" of Christ, going back to the time of his Ascension. When we descended from the mount, we paused at the tomb of Melechai and Hezekiah, the Church of Dominus Flavit, where Jesus wept for Jerusalem, and the site of Gethsemane with those fantastic, ancient olive trees. Some may well be old enough to have witnessed Christ's solitary distress in prayer the night before he suffered.

After returning at last in the evening to Ecce Homo, we studied the *lithostratos*, that is, the stone pavement upon which Christ is believed to have been scourged. We also noted the maze of tunnels that had been constructed directly under our rooms. We concelebrated a Mass in the Ecce Homo Church and then we dined with the Sisters, including a Sister from the Loretto Sisters of India, and had warm chocolate with the religious studies group downstairs. The group took Father Jim and me into the new city for ice cream—which is hardly what we needed this evening. There, in the new city, Father Jim called his father for a birthday greeting. Then we returned to our rooms at 10:30 in the evening, exhausted by the day.

## Mass in the Sepulcher

MARCH 3, TUESDAY

It was a day of writing postcards, buying souvenirs, and praying in a variety of chapels and churches. The interesting aspect of this day was that we were able to obtain a ticket to celebrate Mass tomorrow in the Sepulcher.

Tomorrow is Ash Wednesday. When we first asked about the possibility of having Mass there, the caretaker laughed, stating that the Sepulcher is reserved long in advance. Certainly for Ash Wednesday, the beginning of Lent, it would be impossible to find an open spot one day in advance. Nevertheless, as we were walking out, he ran out after us and informed us that, suddenly, yes, there was an opening! He said that we could, in fact, have a 6:00 A.M. Mass in the Sepulcher! "How is that possible?" I asked. To which he replied that they had just received a phone call telling them that the priest who was to have said Mass tomorrow morning has died. So we resolved to reserve the Mass and remember the priest as one of our intentions for it.

MARCH 4, ASH WEDNESDAY

A cloudy and mild day in the city. We rose early and set out to concelebrate our 6:00 A.M. Mass in the little tomb, the tiny cave from which Christ rose. It was an extraordinary event, because the Mass, of course, makes present the Risen Christ sacramentally in our worship. However, every Mass is actually held in the "empty tomb," just as every Mass is offered from the Upper Room.

## On the Road Again

By 8:30 this morning we had boarded our bus to Tiberius. We rode to the vast plains of Jericho some seventy feet below sea level where man's earliest cities (circa 7000+ B.C.) rose by a great spring.

The wildflower meadows here are in rich bloom. We arrived at the Sea of Galilee at 11:30 A.M.

We are going backwards; we should have come from Galilee to Jerusalem if we wished to follow the temporal sequence of Christ's journey. Nevertheless, there is a certain atemporal sequence in Christ in which one can move backward and forward along the way of his journey with almost equal meaning and ease. In fact, the stories we have of the travels of Jesus to Jerusalem are stories which were written from the perspective of his Crucifixion and Resurrection, so that all of Christ's recorded words and deeds are infused with these mysteries. Perhaps that is why Jesus told his disciples that he would meet them back in Galilee again after his Resurrection. They were then able to reassimilate the meaning of all he had said and done in view of his Paschal mission.

We lunched along the shore on "St. Peter's fish," as it is called. Then we walked through the town by the Crusaders' wall and the towers there, by the Church of St. Peter's Boat, some natural hot springs, and some local shops. We had a vegetarian dinner at a Chinese restaurant where one of the employees tried to start a fire in the hearth because it was so cold. We stayed in the Scottish Hospice, Room No. 44.

## Winding Down

### MARCH 5, THURSDAY

Today we took a tour of the Golan Heights. An officer of the United Nations, whom I had met in Egypt, escorted us through some otherwise restricted areas of the Lebanese-Israeli border, the so-called "good fence" where Lebanese workers had crossed. We saw evidence of recent conflicts and battles, with wreckage strewn along the highway.

We returned to Tiberius early, skipping a nature walk at Tel Dan because of rain, and at Tiberius we caught the 4:00 bus back to Jerusalem. We had our 7:00 P.M. dinner back at Ecce Homo, then concelebrated Mass with the Sisters there.

All told, we paid only $178 for our accommodations, meals, and services in Israel—a minor coup. Sister Rose, also on pilgrimage, brought us brandy so we would sleep well before departing early in the morning for Egypt, and because it is so cold.

MARCH 6, FRIDAY

> *O God of the Universe,*
>
> *Be praised for the mysteries you reveal! So far as I can tell, ours is the only planet where eyes look upward to the heavens to seek you. And in this world, this is the only land wherein you revealed your Word, your face, and your love. I cannot grasp the meaning of it: how you chose one lineage to bless many nations; how you made one land holy beyond all others; how the few whom you call to yourself must be the source of inspiration and enlightenment for the many; how the one you call your Son is the center of your children's life.*
>
> *But I sense that by the nature you created in us, we also center ourselves around the special, the few, and the only. We live through those few who fill our media, provide our entertainment, sing our music, play our games, wear our fashions, rule our realms, write our novels, and parade our wealth. We complain to you about the scandal of your choosing one people and blessing one land, but that is our way too!*
>
> *We cannot find blessing except through the blessed ones held up before our eyes. And the blessed ones themselves find their grace in One more beloved yet. Rather than be scandalized, may I rejoice that you find us through them, and founded them upon him whom you have eternally loved.*
>
> *I have lived to see what his eyes saw when he walked upon the land you promised Israel. The shapes and sights which impress the eyes may likewise compel the mind to engage in thoughts similar to his. As I see what he saw, turn my thoughts to his. You have made this land a sacred trust till we learn to occupy all lands in peace. Give Jerusalem peace!*

## The Holy Tree

MARCH 8, SUNDAY

Back in Egypt, Father Jim and I arrived for the 8:30 A.M. Mass at St. Fatima Church in Heliopolis, an outlying district of Cairo. That particular Mass was prayed in Coptic, although it is a church in which the Eucharist is celebrated in a variety of rites. The bishop who resides near here is Chaldean; he is the bishop of all of the Chaldeans who live in Africa and Egypt. He invited us to tea after Mass and offered us free use of his church.

We returned to the home of the Kamal-Hanna family, with whom I usually stay when in Cairo. Later on that morning we rode with their son Emil to Martariyah, another district of Cairo that boasts of what the Copts call, "The Holy Tree." It is another place that was visited by the Holy Family. The tree is reputed to have grown from the broken staff of Joseph, the husband of Mary, while the family was in flight. Actually, the original tree was cut down long ago and a large, dead substitute of the original sycamore still remains, propped up by poles all around it. Emil suggested that this seventeenth-century tree is, nevertheless, the original, and that it has been carbon-dated to be over two thousand years old. Perhaps it is related somehow to a much older tree. The district surrounding the Holy Tree is in one of the poorest and saddest areas of Cairo.

We visited the Church of St. Mary in Harat Zuwalia where Jesus is said to have uncovered a well from an ancient Pharaonic cave. The water is considered to be a source of blessing, although it might also be the cause of illness, as many birds fly loose in this and other Egyptian churches. Our tour guide claims the church to be eighteen hundred years old, but other sources date it from the tenth century, with heavy renovations in more recent times.

We drove past a truck of militant prisoners denouncing Mubarak, Egypt's president, and urging Islamic revolution. We were stuck in the traffic jam caused by Mubarak's motorcade. He is apparently hosting the president of Uganda. Emil went on to the cathedral for a minute to check my mail box, but failed to recover any messages for me there. We left Emil to his work at the hotel and walked on to St. Fatima Church where we concelebrated an early evening Mass.

## Sharing Our Pilgrimage

MARCH 10, TUESDAY

I spent the first part of the day in the Patriarchate dispensing rosaries, medals, and various other small souvenirs from the Holy Land to many of the workers whom I had befriended in my early months here. They were all eager to hear about our experiences in the Holy Land. The Copts are tremendously interested in holy places. Many of their parents and grandparents went off to the Holy Land on pilgrimage, but for the last several decades it has been impossible for the Copts to travel there due to the tensions between the Israeli government and the Arab world. Indeed, Pope Shenouda has prudently forbidden them to travel to Palestine.

## A Coptic Saint

MARCH 11, WEDNESDAY

Emil and I took Father Jim and two friends of ours to the airport where we bade him our fond farewells.

Immediately after leaving Father Jim, we went to the Hotel Beirut where Mr. Tewfik gathered us into his little car and he, Emil, and I drove the agricultural road north from Cairo to Tanta. One of the tires blew out along the way. Some travelers stopped to help us, but it took a bit of time to fix the tire. As a result, we arrived at Deir Mari Mina around 3:30 or 4:00 in the afternoon. This is a monastery in the desert just south of Alexandria. Bishop Mina, the *kommos* of the monastery, welcomed us very cordially. While Emil conferred with him and Mr. Tewfik, Brother Bessan presented relics and holy cards to me for my veneration.

We then visited the tomb of His Holiness, Pope Kyrillos VI, and spent the rest of the day at the monastery. Pope Kyrillos is regarded as a saint in the Coptic Church, and there are always many pilgrims visiting the spot where he is buried. The tomb is covered with books and tablets and notes of students who have come here seeking his intercession for their academic life. They come either in advance of their exams to ask his help or they come afterwards to thank him for his assistance. When they give thanks, they leave a token of gratitude in these textbooks and notebooks which are strewn all about the place. I cannot help but think of sites in Europe where pilgrims leave signs of their gratitude for the saints' intercession. There are many monasteries, chapels, shrines, and grottos where pilgrims have left their crutches, their bandages, and every possible sign of their former afflictions or illnesses in gratitude for the saints' help. These are rather primal, universal impulses of faith which modern theologians and liturgists disdain at the peril of dehumanizing our religion.

## *Of Building Bonds and Breaking Bondage*

MARCH 12, THURSDAY

After the day at Deir Mari Mina, Mr. Tewfik drove me back along the desert highway to the Monastery of St. Bishoi where the monks were very happy to welcome me back after my absence of a couple of weeks. They always seem warmer to me with each visit than before, because, as one monk explained, now I am free to remain in some other place or some other monastery. I have come to know Egypt well enough to circulate as I like and, had I desired to leave St. Bishoi Monastery, I could have done so. At first I was not so free; it was the place where I had been instructed to stay. But, since I have come back, it must be because I want to. The monks are welcoming me back because they feel that I desire to spend my time with them. All true.

## *Monastic Vocations*

MARCH 18, WEDNESDAY

I have been discussing with a number of the younger monks here the effects of their vocation on their natural families. The general impression is that the family is weakened by their monastic vocation because it fundamentally entails a renunciation of the bonds of family life. They leave their father and their mother; they leave their home, their brothers and sisters. They leave their lineage, as well as the aunts and uncles and grandparents who are almost always living nearby. In doing so, it is regarded as an assault on their family and it causes great grief. Moreover, in choosing to be celibate, they are renouncing the possibility of a future marriage. There may even be a particular woman preselected by their parents whom they are choosing not to marry (or with whom they are choosing not to pursue a relationship which could possibly lead to marriage). Their filial bonds, paternal bonds, sibling bonds, and marital bonds are all seemingly undermined by their vocation.

But several of the monks told me that these roles are actually undermined all the time by the utterly selfish manner in which they are often assumed in the secular world. People very often marry, have children, and maintain relationships in their families for reasons of prestige, or for reasons of control and power. They often humiliate others and subjugate them to their will. Or they marry out of their insecurities and their needs which must be met by others. They marry to fulfill themselves through others. In all of this, seeking the good of the other is not the primary goal of many family men. Consequently, without the religious life witnessing to something transcendent, family life could be eroded.

By sacrificing the goals of prestige and control and power, by sacrificing even the desire to fulfill himself and to address his insecurities, the monk concretizes great values. He evidences the virtue of humility by his submission to God's will; he exercises the virtue of charity by his service to others and by placing the needs of others above his own. His heart and mind are sanctified by the worship that he continuously gives to God. These values ultimately infuse not only the monastery, but also the Church the monastery serves and, therefore, all the families of that Church. All people who come as pilgrims to the monastery are blessed by the reinforcement of these values. All readers of monastic hagiography, all those who were ever romanced by the ideals or the reality of the monastery are enriched by the vocation of the monk. Therefore, the families of the Church in Egypt are ultimately strengthened, even if in some immediate sense they are seemingly weakened by this or that particular monastic vocation.

In addition, it occurred to me that, in terms of an anthropological analysis, while the monk's vocation to a monastery seemingly trivializes secular life and diminishes the value of self-seeking relationships or merely natural family relationships, it simultaneously inverts the wealth, the status, and the prestige of the secular world. That is, by what he sacrifices he shows the relative value of his vocation; he demonstrates the proportional level of his commitment.

That is why monasteries frequently boast about members who have given up much to enter. The would-be engineer or physician may have lost his worldly position, but the magnitude of the monk's sacrifice becomes his ultimate success. Those who give up much seemingly lose much, but, in the loss, they obtain for themselves and for their monastery a different kind of wealth: the prestige of great self-donation by which the value of the alternative social order of the Church is reinforced.

## *Springs in the Desert*

MARCH 20, FRIDAY

A certain Palestinian Christian by the name of Mr. Raymon came to visit St. Bishoi Monastery. He is an agricultural specialist who has come to assess the quality of the agriculture on the monastic farm. The farm is watered by so-called "fossil water," pumped out of the floor of the Sahara Desert. It is water from a very old branch of the Nile River which must have flowed nearer to this part of the desert in ancient times.

Mr. Raymon took me with him and I have spent all day accompanying him on his inspection of the agricultural plant, as well as one on a nearby plot of land recently acquired by the monastery. I discovered that there is a water trench right behind the stables I had not known about and I learned more about the agriculture of this monastery's farm in one day than I had in several months of my own observation.

One fact that has slowly dawned on me is that Coptic monasteries occupy the best well-water zones in the Sahara Desert. This is, in part, because the monks have been here for so long that they have had time to locate the places best suited for human habitation. Aside from that, there were once thousands, perhaps tens of thousands of monks living in the desert in the earliest years of monasticism. They would have lived over such a wide geographic area that eventually some of them would have discovered the best freshwater reserves in the Sahara. Then, as the population of the monasteries decreased and as the monks clustered in fewer and fewer places, they would have chosen to congregate near the best springs of water, near the best places from which to draw water to cultivate their gardens.

The process seems to me sensible enough, almost like an evolutionary movement, and it is all the more striking, then, for me to hear the monastic interpretation of their present locations. The monks describe themselves as having come to this or that particular place because their founding abbot was led to that exact spot by an angel. They believe that the first abbot planted a staff there and that his staff became a tree, or that he scooped out some sand and the hole became a spring. Their location is spoken of almost entirely in terms of the theological setting of the monastery and its place in God's Providence, rather than in terms of its infrastructural or ecological position. I think that the monastic explanation is every bit as valid as my Western interpretation. I like it better; it communicates more and, in its own way, is as accurate as it is descriptive.

## Ecumenical Gestures

MARCH 23, MONDAY

This is the first truly hot day of the year and today Abuna Demetria brought me a black cap to wear under my hood! Of course, here in the desert, my hood is always worn up, as it is considered appropriate for monks to cover their heads. In the West, monks rarely wear their hoods up, maybe only when it's cold, or in Lent. But Abuna Demetria and the various monks here want me to have the proper "look" of a monk in a Coptic monastery.

It's an interesting thing to me how their concern about the proper "look" inspires them to address me. From the beginning, the Coptic Pope asked me to grow a beard so that I would not look out of place. Then, of course, I had to wear my hood up so that I would not confuse the visitors to the monastery as to what kind of monk allows his head to be uncovered. They gave me a wooden hand-cross so that I could give blessings in a manner which the pilgrims would understand, even though I am not a Coptic Orthodox priest or monk. Yet they wanted me to give blessings—an ecumenical gesture which was not lost on me. I wonder, indeed, how many Orthodox Churches in Europe would provide a visiting priest with a hand-cross to give blessings in their monasteries in a manner that their people can appreciate. In all of these ways, the Coptic monks emphasize a certain degree of regard for proper decorum among Religious and priests, so that, by external signs, graces are provided to the faithful.

At the same time, they have extended to me an ecumenical acceptance—on a primal level, to be sure, because there are many difficulties between the Churches—but they assert a basic ecumenical unity which I find very heartening. However, as heartening as all of this is, I'm also appreciative of the irony of wearing a black wool cap under my hood only as the weather turns hot!

This irony is all the sweeter because it also provides me an opportunity to experience something of the discomfort that Religious women in the West experienced for centuries in covering their heads, even when the weather was hot, and doing so with multiple layers. Religious men in the West, as well as diocesan clergy and the laity, look back nostalgically at the advantages of having Religious Sisters in full habit, including veils. Now, at last, I have a chance to appreciate what this must have felt like.

## The Prodigal Son

MARCH 28, SATURDAY

Today I met with Abuna Elia to talk about the parables of Jesus. We discussed at length The Story of the Prodigal Son, which is a Lenten meditation for many of the monks here. They like to point out that the prodigal son was suffering from a kind of incurable illness because the nature of habitual sin and weakness is like a debilitating disease. Indeed, as Abuna Elia explained, the biblical word, "dissipated," which in the Gospel of St. Luke is used to describe the quality of the second son's moral life, is also a medical term. Yet the father has compassion on him, not so much because he believes the younger son can substantially change, but simply because the younger son is so greatly in need of his compassion. Whether the younger son can change cannot be learned from the story and, in that sense, it reminds us all of our own spiritual lives and conversion process. If we are going to become sanctified, it will not be because we have been able to plan and realize it by our own desire and our own virtue, but because it is a result of God's compassion for us.

Abuna Elia pointed out that the prodigal son is actually a figure of Christ—not because anything is amiss in Christ, but because Jesus has assumed all that is amiss in us. He has absorbed all our sins and all our weaknesses into himself so that he became the victim of all that has dehumanized us and estranged us from God. Therefore, when the father says about the prodigal son, *"He was dead, but now he is alive"* (Luke 15:24), it is descriptive of the state of glory to which Christ has risen and to which we will also one day rise in him. But even now, we rise in him by faith and by grace, inwardly.

Likewise, we are to penitentially identify ourselves with the elder son whose voice of strict justice regarding his younger brother is descriptive of the types of relationships we sometimes have with one another. We often summon others to a degree of justice and virtue greater than that which we ourselves are able to reach. We sometimes hold other people to lofty standards that we ourselves cannot meet.

There is no resolution given to the elder son's predicament in the story either. The father goes out to plead with him and makes an eloquent case, urging him to be sympathetic and compassionate. We are not told whether the elder son follows through or not. Likewise, the question is an open one with us. Yesterday's compassion that we showed to anyone; yesterday's sympathy that we expressed; yesterday's virtues that we evidenced do not really resolve the question as to whether or not our lives shall be summed up in the same way. Our lives cannot be judged as compassionate or loving or kind unless we willingly take up the same yoke again and again each and every day.

## Workers in the Vineyard

MARCH 29, SUNDAY

Abuna Elia and I met today in the garden between Deir el Suriani and Deir Anba Bishoi. There are orange trees growing in this garden; the scent of the orange blossoms is very sweet just now, so Abuna Elia wanted to meet there in the shade.

We sat and discussed another parable, the story of the workers in the vineyard. Abuna Elia pointed out that the owner of the vineyard came to the marketplace, the appropriate place to hire workers. He came there early in the morning, in the middle of the morning, and at noon. He came again in mid-afternoon and even in the late afternoon to hire anyone who was still there. He combed through that place again and again and rightly knew that had anyone been there all day, he would have seen him on one of his frequent visits. And yet when he came in the late afternoon, he said to those who had come there only lately, *"Why have you been standing here all day in the hot sun? Go you also to my vineyard"* (cf. Matthew 20:6-7).

He asked them that question, even though he knew they had not been standing there all day. Perhaps they had slept in that morning or had lounged about. Perhaps they had had a leisurely lunch somewhere, or they had taken a walk with their friends. Perhaps they had had coffee someplace (as it were) and lazed through the afternoon. Then, fearing to come home without an explanation, they went to the marketplace *as if* they had been available to hire themselves out. But, of course, who would hire anyone in the last hour, literally, of the workday? Since that would be highly unlikely, going to the marketplace at that hour would simply provide an excuse for why they had not worked at all. Such a person could then say to his wife, "I went to the marketplace and no one hired me."

"How big do you imagine a village marketplace could be," Abuna Elia asked, "that these would-be laborers were somehow overlooked in the earlier visits? No, they were as we are, largely unavailable to divine commerce.

"When the owner of the vineyard came to the marketplace late in the day, he asked the laborers a question that granted them a dignity they did not deserve. He addressed them as if they had been searching for employment for a much longer time than they actually had.

"What does that mean?" Abuna Elia asked, "—except that, analogously, God knows that, deep within our souls, we have been searching for him and seeking to please him all our lives, even though we have seemingly been avoiding doing just that. When we have been lazy or distracted or otherwise preoccupied, nevertheless, it was our deepest desire to seek God. And so, when he approaches us, he speaks to us as if we had been in the marketplace all day, waiting to be hired. He addresses us as if we had been actively seeking him, searching for love, aspiring for goodness, open to grace. He says to us, 'Where have you been? Why are you not in my vineyard?' Without stripping us of our dignity, without humiliating us, he invites us to come, providing for us the proper context for our dialogue with him. He alludes to his awareness of our deepest desire to be with him.

"When they came to the vineyard, the latecomers surely must have realized that there were many workers already there who had been hired much earlier. They must have realized that the owner of the vineyard had no real need to bring them in at the last moment, but that he was seeking a pretext whereby he could be generous. Indeed, when he put them first in line, and then gave them a full day's wage, they must have been crushed by his kindness. He did not humiliate them by his judgment; he humbled them by his compassion."

By having the owner of the vineyard give the latecomers a full day's wage, Christ implies that he has no restrictions, no limits to the love he wishes to give us, in spite of our sins. He wishes to supply us with the fullness of his friendship or, as Abuna Elia always says, "baptism into communion—a communion which is no less for the one who comes at the eleventh hour than for the one who has been in the vineyard all day."

Of course, I raised the constant objection to the apparent injustice in this parable: the injustice of the workers who came last being given the same wage as those who came first. Abuna Elia pointed out, "This is an injustice only for those whose heart is small, who cannot enjoy the paradox of those who have come late being welcomed into the same friendship which they have always enjoyed. It is a great mystery. They were invited to be members of the master's vineyard from the beginning of their lives, early on in the day. They were allowed to be co-workers with his own, to be a part of his household all day. All day long they knew their wage was coming; all day long they knew that they were welcomed and accepted, that they belonged. They were not suffering the tortures of the unemployed, those who had not found refuge, acceptance, security, or purpose. They had found it early and retained it long. If they wish to perceive this as slavery and drudgery in the hot sun, as we sometimes tend to view our spiritual lives, that is up to them. But it is only by God's grace that our hearts were opened, that we were welcomed into the vineyard, into the work of the Lord, to begin with."

### Ceremonial Preparations

MARCH 30, MONDAY

There are many guests in the monastery now: priests and bishops from all over Egypt and even beyond its borders. Coptic Orthodox clergy have descended on the monastery by the dozens because they are about to begin the ceremony whereby the Sacred Myron, the holy chrism of the Coptic Church, is consecrated.

I was honored to be part of the hospitality of the monastery in receiving all these guests. The monks gingerly asked me if I would be willing to move from my room on the first floor of the monastery guest house to an upper room, which is virtually in the rafters of the building, so that more senior monks and bishops could have the room I have been using. I was pleased that they felt comfortable enough to ask me to do so, as I've been here long enough that I can take on something of the burden of hospitality with them. But unfortunately, the room which I was given is filled with mosquitoes, so I have to wrestle with them throughout the night!

Apparently, the consecrating of the holy oil is a ritual act which requires a large collection of clerics to be present and which, in fact, takes many days to complete. I am looking forward to observing this. I consider it great good luck to be here in the monastery for the event, especially since it occurs only rarely. There have been periods in Coptic Church history when the oil was consecrated only once or twice in a century. It happens a little more frequently now, and it is highly fortuitous that I am here as an anthropologist to witness and record it.

The oils that are being consecrated will be used for baptism, for confirmation, for the anointing of the sick, and for the ordination of a priest or bishop, as well as for the consecration of the patriarch himself. The fact that the monks are consecrating the oil more frequently nowadays is an indication of its more frequent use, owing to the rising population of the Copts. Now there may be six or seven million of them, whereas a century or two ago there would have been only a few hundred thousand of them.

About twenty-six ingredients to be used in the consecration of the oil were brought to the church today and mixed together. They were carried around the church three times by much of the monastic community, with songs and incense. The newly ordained parish priests who are in residence likewise joined in the procession, as well as the visiting clergy.

During an interlude in the ceremony, Pope Shenouda was interviewed by a U.S. news team, perhaps from CNN. He fielded questions about the role of monasticism in Coptic life and the role of the monastery in the so-called "sectarian strife" of Egypt. He was perhaps uncomfortable in the suggestion that monasteries are somehow players in the increasing sectarian tensions in Egypt, but he answered the questions very diplomatically, hinting that his great respect for the present president of Egypt is greater than his respect for the former one. It seems that he is always trying to make the most of present opportunities, at least over the losses of the past.

After the interview, Pope Shenouda returned to the ritual and began the grinding and the sifting of some of the ingredients while prayers and chants were sung. By 7:30 this evening, he retired to his quarters. However, the ritual process will last about another week.

> *Generous King,*
>
> *You bless and nourish your children on their pilgrimage: "Bread to cheer the heart of man; oil to make his face to shine" (Psalm 104:15). Bread, bread, always the staff of life and the sign of your Providence, but oil is a more mysterious sign of your plan! Upon what nature does this grace build?*
>
> *Is it the use of oil in the preparation of food that you mean to signify to us? Are we anointed with oil because we become one with the Bread of Life you are making of us? Is it the oiling of Greek athletes in advance of Olympic competition, or the rubbing down of runners' limbs when the race is done that you mean to signify? For, surely, we are always anticipating the challenges to come, or recovering from the rigors last endured! Or is it that oil makes moisture abide longer on human skin, so that the waters of our Baptism will remain a present reality to us?*
>
> *But I keep thinking of the oil given to us for the "face to shine." Did you not intend your priests, prophets, and kings of old to shine in the midst of your people? Were they not anointed so that the nation would know that, more than human charisma and popular appeal, it was your light that shone out from them, that your anointing empowered them?*
>
> *A light is set up on a lampstand; a city shines on a hill. A holy man somehow radiates more brightly in the lightless land of the desert and illumines the darkened eyes of his Church. Are the desert monks seemingly hidden here under a bushel basket in their caves? No, the hearts of the faithful, even the impulse of faith in the churchless, hold them up and draw them forth till they, too, shine with the grace of your anointing among us. Alone, silent, and sequestered, the desert monk radiates with your light at the center of the assembly you gather.*

## *A Fly on the Wall*

MARCH 31, TUESDAY

The influx of all the visiting dignitaries and guests provides a wonderful opportunity to be "the fly on the wall" of many conversations. There are visiting prelates from Europe here; two are Coptic Orthodox bishops. Monks are visiting from the States who are in some small Orthodox enclave in communion with the Coptic Church. Clergy from Africa who are part of the Coptic Orthodox missions, as well as bishops and monks from every other monastery and diocese in Egypt have come.

Today I had lunch with a group of these people prepared by the visiting American monks who are from a small monastery in Oklahoma. They are from a constituency of Orthodoxy about which I had no knowledge, but which is somehow in communion with the Coptic Orthodox Church. They prepared a meatless—but meat-like—meal for the guests in our group. Beaming, they said, "It's full of MSG and soybeans, but it's tasty." The meal was prepared by a certain Father Arsenius. The topics discussed over this MSG and soybean meal were very interesting. The monks talked about the nature of ecumenism and how the Coptic Orthodox Church is well situated with its essential conservatism to be a pivotal actor among the various Orthodox Churches and Catholicism.

We discussed monasticism. One Coptic monk stated (if I understood his Arabic correctly) that "the monk's cell is a frying pan." This remark bothered another visiting monk. We discussed the potential loss of Egypt's Coptic diaspora, because once the Copts leave Egypt, it is difficult for them to remain as closely linked to their Church as they had been when they lived here. Also, in many places there are cities and towns without a Coptic Orthodox community. Even if they have a Coptic Orthodox parish to which they can attach themselves, it is difficult for them to raise their children in their Faith since they are exposed to so many counter-religious and secular traditions.

Coptic Orthodoxy has adapted itself to the peculiar tension of passing on the Faith in an Islamic world, even in a hostile Islamic world, but it is not so well adapted to passing itself on in a secular world, especially a world colored by the religious backgrounds of many other Christian denominations. "Somebody must tell Pope

Shenouda more about this," one monk opined. I cannot imagine that Pope Shenouda is not already keenly aware of it.

One monk asked me how I felt about the stigmatist, Anna Catherine Emmerich. Another one told me that he has a picture of Pope Pius XII in his cell, for he considers him to be a great saint. He added that this Pope was so strong in his faith that on one or two occasions he actually raised the dead by prayer. I didn't know about that, but a visiting abbot had heard about it as well.

They wondered about the Oriental practices that have been entering into Western Churches, such as meditation, breathing, and stretching exercises, which are designed to "center" a person. The Coptic Orthodox monks didn't like the idea of being "centered" by techniques, and even if that were possible, they thought it couldn't be as efficacious or important as being centered by faith in the Paschal Mysteries of Christ.

We spoke, then, at length about those mysteries, and our great grace and joy to be invited therein, so the conversation went late. It was nearly midnight when I returned to my room, such as it is, but I wasn't anxious to get back there since I knew it would be a night made fairly sleepless by mosquitoes.

# ☼ APRIL
## A TIME OF CONSECRATION

### *Of Sandstorms and Saintly Abbots*

APRIL 1, WEDNESDAY

A terrific sandstorm blew in this morning. We have entered the so-called "season of the wind," which is part of the Coptic meteorological calendar. Actually, according to the monks here, it's about a week and a half or two overdue. Although it's a terrible storm and there's very little visibility, all the monks and even all the visitors are actually happy about it. It seems that an almost psychological burden has been lifted from them now that the "season of the wind" has finally arrived. They see it as beneficial because it aids the cultivation of the crops in the Nile Valley. Pollination cannot occur, they say, unless the winds are strong.

The papal residence is in walking distance on an estate adjoining the monastery, yet far enough away that in the sandstorm His Holiness will have difficulty in getting here for the initial ritual of the consecration of the Holy Myron. We were told that he should be arriving at 4:00 P.M. near the monastery wall, so we all went out there to meet him. We stood, because it would be impolite to be seated when we greet the Pope. Actually, we stood for four hours until 8:00 in the evening when His Holiness arrived, so much had the sandstorm made transportation difficult! But surely, there must have been more to it than that.

When he finally arrived, the Pope had with him in his car the aged abbot of Deir el Suriani, Anba Tewfilos. He's very old now, and is regarded by many as one of the chief agents of ecclesiastical and monastic restoration in the Coptic Church. He's one of the great figures of the twentieth century who brought a renewal to this Church and a certain new vibrancy to the religious life. Directly or indirectly, his ministry as monk and abbot has been part of the conversion story of many of the present leaders of the Coptic Church. He is regarded as a living saint, even by the monks of his own House. Although he has been living just next door to me for all these months, I have not seen him until now because he has been ill—not actually bedridden, but not out-of-doors, and not meeting any of the guests who come to his monastery. But I will now have a chance to meet him, and I am grateful for this opportunity.

## Of Novices Old and New

Today six aspiring monks were given the white *galabeya* (habit), a sign of their probational acceptance into the monastery. One of them was Brother Wagee who has sometimes been assigned to me on a day-by-day basis to execute any little tasks that I might need to be carried out for my studies. Brother Wagee also brings me messages. If any of the monks here wish to meet with me, or if they want to provide insights, they often send word through Brother Wagee. So I was glad to see that today he was formally accepted to begin his monastic life. In addition, several new novices have come recently to begin discerning their vocation.

The old novices, those about to become monks, will now spend the day and the coming night in prayer in the monastic church. They will be given a new name tomorrow at their monastic consecration. As they spend the night in the church, they will be visited by their brother monks, one by one, who will "give them a word" to assist them, to direct them, to guide them, for the rest of their monastic life. It's a wonderful idea. The novices are quite excited about this night of visitation, the night in which they will receive all at once, by the good will and the wisdom of their older brothers, all that they will need for their formation henceforth. Pope Shenouda has already indicated that one of the novices will be given the name "Myron," that is, he is to be named after the Holy Myron, since the monastic consecration will coincide with the consecration of the holy oils of the Coptic Church. A great deal is happening all at once, it seems, deep in the heart of Lent in this monastery.

*Grass mats cover the floor of a monk's cell.*

Just as in the monasteries of the West, the novices leaving the Novitiate and the new ones coming in have overlapping identities for one day, so there's a special kinship ascribed to them as though they were all one class. They are even photographed as a class. It reminds me vividly of the same phenomenon which occurs in my own monastery at St. Vincent: the photographing of two classes together because, for one day, they are all novices together. The new ones get to imagine what they soon will be; the old ones get to reminisce about what they once were. The aspiration for the monastic life is reinforced for each class, because, at this time, their identities coincide.

This evening, some of the ingredients for the Holy Myron were mixed. In particular, a kind of wood pulp was left to soak for twelve hours. The cells of the wood will expand in the water in which it was placed, and that substance will be added to boiling oil tomorrow. Then the ritual will properly commence.

### Monastic Consecration

APRIL 2, THURSDAY

At 7:30 this morning, I witnessed the rite of monastic consecration for the six old novices. At the beginning of the rite, they were simply told to lie down on their backs while pillows were placed under their heads. Then they were covered with the shroud which ordinarily covers the relics of their founder, St. Bishoi. The dirges of Holy Week, especially those of Good Friday, were sung, as well as the litanies of the saints from their funerals. Passages from the Old Testament were read: the call of Abraham; the second chapter of the Book of Sirach which talks about how one must be prepared for trials if he comes to serve the Lord, as well as other texts.

From time to time, Pope Shenouda lifted up the large shroud which covered the novices to let a little air ventilate the place where they were resting. The monks whispered to me that this is an uncommon act of kindness from His Holiness, inasmuch as it is thought to be part of the ritual of monastic consecration to let those who are about to be consecrated "simmer," on the dark, hot, shroud-covered floor of the church. Indeed, according to some of the monks, in the more remote past, it sometimes happened that monks died of heat prostration during the many hours of the ceremony. Even recently, some monks passed out during the ritual, so grievous is the weight of the shroud, the lack of air, and the accumulation of body warmth.

There were no words which the monks being consecrated had to say, no other ritual they had to perform. They just had to lie there under the shroud. The rite of consecration was accomplished effectively by the songs and the prayers of the monks who were all around them in the church. Apparently, the willingness of the monks being consecrated simply to lie there manifested their full supplication of heart and mind and will to live the monastic life. They "died" to the world outside the monastery; that is why they lay there under the funereal shroud. This is not altogether different from the ceremony held in many monasteries in the Western Church which have traditionally performed their monastic consecration the same way, even until recent times.

So important is the funereal aspect of monastic solemn consecration in Egypt that, I am told, for monks of olden times, no funeral masses were said for them when they died. Rather, they were simply buried, because their funeral had taken place on the day of their consecration and did not need to be repeated after their death!

At the end of the ceremony, the shroud was lifted and all six monks rose up, thanks be to God. They were tonsured and then they were named. They were rapidly vested in the black *galabeya* of the traditional desert monk and were given the stitched cap which the monks have been wearing for the last generation or so. In prior times they simply wore a black wool cap over their heads, but now they wear a hood-like cowl stitched with twelve crosses.

I'm not familiar with all of the varieties of religious garments in the Eastern or Orthodox Churches generally, but I think this matches a type of hood worn in other Oriental Churches. Pope Shenouda introduced this style to bring the Egyptian Church into greater participation with the larger ecclesiastical world.

The twelve crosses, representing the twelve apostles, are sewn into the hood. They are to remind the monks that by their withdrawal into the desert, their solitude, and their private prayer, they are nevertheless living an apostolic life. They are providing life to the apostolic labors of their Church by giving her a contemplative heart. The cowl is made of two pieces of black fabric which are sewn together by cross-stitches of a different color, so it can be clearly seen that the cowl has been made from two pieces of cloth.

When I asked about the meaning of this stitch work, I was told that it signifies that the monk, like the hood, is rent in two. He is separated from the world, the world in which he had deep attachments, and he is separated from his own appetites, his own desires and his own will. The monk is always being divided. Jesus said, *"I have come to make division"* (Luke 12:51). The monks say that they are the ones in whom the division is the most graphic because they have been separated out of the world by their consecration and by their solitary prayer. *"Kadosh"* in Hebrew and *"Kodes"* in Arabic both convey a sense that holiness is a process of separation from worldly absorption.

### *Of English Bibles and Coptic Rituals*

Pope Shenouda was particularly joyous today. He invited me into the sanctuary and asked to borrow my English Bible so that he could read one or two of the passages from it on behalf of the English-speaking prelates who are present as guests. He told me once that he likes to use English in the Coptic ritual, since there is nothing in particular about the Arabic language that is essential to Coptic ritual. He said that if it is not being read in Coptic, the language of the ancient Pharaohs, it may just as well be read in English. I wonder whether he is content to use a language other than the language of the Koran because, of course, the Koran has so completely formed the Arabic language. He did not say this, nor would he be likely to say so if asked. Nevertheless, Arabic is essential to Islam and only peripheral to Coptic Christianity.

### *Impressions of America*

Somehow in the midst of all of this commotion, His Holiness took me aside for another walk around the edge of the monastery. He spoke to me about his journey to America, from which he had just returned, and his impressions of Christianity in America. He told me how grateful he is that the Catholic Church in the States has been so solicitous for the welfare of the Coptic Orthodox diaspora who are distributed everywhere in our country. Catholic priests and, indeed, many Christian clergy are allowing the Copts to use their churches and other facilities, many times almost free of charge.

## Coptic Vessels

APRIL 3, FRIDAY

For most of the day, the Sacred Myron was simply settling, so there was not too much ritual activity. I met with several of the bishops of the Coptic Orthodox Church. By now I know more Coptic Orthodox bishops than Catholic prelates. One in particular asked to see what kinds of vessels I am using to celebrate the Catholic Mass. When I showed him my Mass kit, such as it is, he graciously offered to lend me another one with vessels of Coptic vintage. From one of his attendants he produced a wooden box containing various icons, an altar cloth, and sacred vessels for the celebration of the Mass. He said that when I was finished with my work in Egypt I could mail the box back to him. A very gracious gift which I assured him I would use. With a little bit of adaptation, it's perfectly assimilable to the Catholic Mass, especially as I pray it here.

## The Process Continues

APRIL 4, SATURDAY

At 9:00 this morning, new ingredients were added to the Myron and it was reheated amid much stirring. Various prelates, priests and monks were invited to participate in the stirring. It is an arduous task, as it must be done continuously all day today. At the same time, it is regarded as an honor to be invited. A variety of Scripture texts were read as part of the process. The wisdom of God's Word is somehow regarded as being mixed in with the oil so that those to be anointed with it will likewise be anointed with the Word of God.

My great thrill today was the invitation of Pope Shenouda to read one of the Scripture texts while the oil was being stirred. I read from the First Book of Kings, chapter 19, verses 9 to 18. In these verses, Elijah encounters God on the Mountain of Horeb and he is enjoined to anoint two kings in Israel, as well as a prophet to succeed him. That is to say, the greatest consequence of the divine epiphany experienced by Elijah on the Mount of Horeb involved the use of oil. This is similar to the epiphany through which Christ, at the Father's right hand, is continuously empowering the Church to use oil in her sacramental life: to baptize, to confirm, to heal, to prepare someone to die, to consecrate priests for the service of the altar.

Those in attendance were somewhat surprised that I had been invited to read and thus participate so intimately in the rite. No one could remember a Catholic priest ever being asked to take part in this way and I feel very honored, indeed, to have been invited. The Pope has been very kind to me throughout my visit, and has been particularly generous today.

After my reading of the Scripture, I retired to the guest house. I met a monk from Ethiopia who speaks English, so we discussed monastic life in his country. He told me that there are hundreds of monasteries in Ethiopia and that he himself had been raised in one of them. He said that in some of the monasteries the diet is very austere. For instance, in one place, they only eat bananas mashed in fish. Most monks eat only once a day there. I'm fascinated by his description of these monasteries, and he insisted that one day I must make a study of monasticism there, just as I am doing in Egypt.

### Are You Still Here?

APRIL 5, SUNDAY

After the morning Kodes, I went to the monastery keep, the fortress adjacent to the guest house, for my private Mass. The two Syrian monks who are visiting here came to observe my Liturgy and were very enthusiastic about it.

After my Mass, I was captured by very large numbers of Coptic Christians who are coming as pilgrims to the monastery these days. They beseeched me for a blessing and it was difficult to get away. I was finally able to evade them by running into the papal residence, where the guard keeps the pilgrims from entering.

In the papal compound I met a certain gentleman named Nasr Hakim, a nephew of Mr. Tewfik, the owner of the hotel I have visited in Cairo. Nasr is from Khartoum and works in the importing and exporting of lumber. He told me about the suffering of the Christians in the Sudan and said that the situation there is deteriorating. In the next few years he imagines that there will be much loss of Christian life in that country. This is not something about which I am at all familiar at present, so I listened attentively to his descriptions of the situation there.

I also had another opportunity to meet Bishop Serapion, the secretary of Pope Shenouda and the bishop in charge of Ecumenical Affairs. He is always observing what I am doing and asking questions about my progress. Anba Serapion questioned me, in a gentle way, about my need to stay so long in Egypt. He doesn't fully understand the "participant-observation" requirement of the anthropologist, although I have tried to explain to him that the intensity of the process requires about a year of sustained presence.

He keeps imagining that I am trying to learn something of the art and the spirit of monasticism in Egypt so that I can transplant it to the States. He told me that American culture would not permit monasticism such as it is practiced in Egypt, that my country is antithetical to this kind of monasticism. I neither agreed nor disagreed with him. I'm not sure to what kind of monasticism American culture would be agreeable. I feel that even to live Benedictine monasticism in America is already something so countercultural that most of us who are trying to do so are unconsciously compromised in many of our efforts, inasmuch as we are as much the children of our culture as we are the sons of St. Benedict. So if *we*, who are Western Religious and have been living in Western culture for all these centuries, are compromised, it may well be that the mentality of Eastern monasticism could not easily be transplanted into the States.

## To Visit or To Stay?

I had a two-hour conversation with Pope Shenouda this afternoon. He told me about new buildings that are being constructed in the papal compound and in the Monastery of St. Bishoi. He talked about the need for a spirit of calm amongst his people: that they

must never allow themselves to become excited by any of the difficulties they must endure in the face of persecution. He spoke about
the need for a greater revival of the Coptic Church. He is grateful
to God for the revival that he has seen throughout his lifetime during which he has participated as a layman in his Sunday school
work, then as a monk, as a priest, and now as Pope.

He asked me about my own family, about my parents and my
brothers and sisters. When I told him that I am one of nine children, he reminded me of the family of St. Basil and his ten siblings.
He said that he imagines my family must be blessed with sanctity,
since he has somehow gotten a good impression of it from knowing
me. I told him that I am the least religious of us all, but that my
family home is indeed a holy place. I am constantly impressed by
the graces I have observed in my parents and in my brothers and
sisters.

"Would you want to stay in the monastery here rather than return to the United States at the end of your research year?" he
asked me. It wasn't an impertinent question; he meant it gently,
simply saying that he was not requiring me to depart at any particular time. He noted that I seem to be very much at home in the
monastery. Indeed, many of the monks, as well as many of the
bishops and prelates visiting the monastery at this time, seem to be
able to speak to me easily. He noted that I am fairly able to integrate myself among them. Pope Shenouda's question about staying
here indefinitely contrasts with Anba Serapion's question about
why I stay here so long. Both are good questions, perhaps even two
aspects of the same question.

Today, the ambassador from France as well as a German theological group came to visit St. Bishoi Monastery. The group was
unable to meet with His Holiness, so I was all the more honored
that I had an opportunity to talk with him at such length.

### Coptic Baptism

This was also "Baptism Sunday" in the monastery. Many guests
came to the monastery today and brought their newborns to be
baptized. Babies—that is, boys at the age of forty days, and girls at
the age of eighty days—are usually baptized in the Coptic Church

in their own home parish. Otherwise, when they are close to those ages, they are brought to the monasteries which are considered to be especially auspicious locations for the Sacrament of Baptism.

The children are anointed with holy oil in thirty-six different locations on their bodies: the eyes, the nose, the mouth, the ears, the armpits, the inner side of the elbows, the underside of the knees, and so on; thirty-six locations which correspond in the Coptic folk way of reckoning the thirty-six openings or portals of the body. By the sacramental baptism they are receiving, these portals must be anointed, that is, opened to the grace of God and closed to everything that is evil. The baptized must then always guard the opening of their heart and mind, as well as the openings of their body.

The Church, likewise, must guard its openings, its portals: the places where good comes in or goes out; the places where evil comes in or goes out. These sites must be given over to the Providence of God and the protection of his good Spirit. The anointing of the individual child is a moment of blessing in the Church's public life. It is a sign that she keeps herself always guarded against the incursions of the outside world in all the places where she is vulnerable. So I reflect that my presence here, and especially my commentary from here, places me at one portal of Coptic communal life. I must be "anointed" with sensitivity for my hosts.

### Useful Contacts

APRIL 6, MONDAY

It seems that a very large part of the Coptic clergy is here. Many monks and almost all of the bishops and abbots of the Church are also present. Today, during the stirring of the Myron, I had the chance to meet most of the visiting abbots. Each one of them, in his turn, personally invited me to come to his House to continue my studies there. If I were to stay as long as each of them has invited me, I would be in Egypt another year or two! Nevertheless, it is good for me to make contact with them now, so that when I do visit them, they will already be familiar with me and my work. This will make it easier for me to enter more fully into my research when I go to their monasteries, God willing, in the future.

I was asked yet again to do a reading during the consecration of the Myron, this time from the first chapter of the Acts of the Apostles, verses 1 to 14. In this passage, Jesus, just before his Ascension, instructs his disciples to remain in Jerusalem till they are baptized by the Holy Spirit. This "baptism" of Pentecost is an anointing, said the Pope, an outpouring of grace which empowers the Church to anoint with oil in the Name of Jesus.

Even more ingredients were added and stirred into the oil today, and the fire was heated to a higher temperature. It seems that the volume of the oil has been melting down and diminishing a bit during these days of consecration, but I'm told that this is as it should be.

## Midnight Watch

APRIL 7, TUESDAY

I rose in the middle of the night and accompanied one of the priests, Abuna Girgus, into the church to strain the Myron, to add new ingredients, and then to fire the charcoal. I was privileged to do this. Abuna Girgus is something of a chemist; he wanted to show me some of the technical parts of the ceremony so that I would understand it better in terms of my research.

During the day, balsam was added to the oil and passages from 1 Corinthians, chapters 12 to 14 were read, dealing with the gifts of the Holy Spirit. Many bishops participated again today. This seems to be the day of greatest participation of those from outside the House. I dined in the papal residence again in their company. Bishop Serapion, who has come and gone and returned again from Cairo, brought me a bundle of mail which had arrived at the Patriarchate for me.

## An Ethiopian Seminarian

APRIL 8, WEDNESDAY

An Ethiopian seminarian named Bekalu, with whom I have been in contact, is studying in Cairo at the Patriarchate seminary. He arrived today for the ceremony with some Ethiopian monks.

After greeting me he told me that he had received word from St. Vincent Seminary that his application has been accepted to attend there perhaps next year. I'm trying to assist him in getting a scholarship to study at our seminary, as well as to translate his transcripts into something that can be integrated into our curriculum. I don't know how possible this will be, but I can see that it is his earnest desire that it be done.

Even Pope Shenouda has indicated that he would be grateful if this could be arranged. It is difficult for Coptic students to get permission from the Pope to study in seminaries outside the Orthodox and the Coptic world, so I am surprised by this particular permission. Perhaps His Holiness thinks that my monastery would be a better place of study for a Coptic Orthodox seminarian—or, in this case, an Ethiopian Orthodox seminarian—than one of which he has no knowledge.

### A Host of Readers

I had dinner with monks from Syria today and then was driven with Pope Shenouda, in his own car, back to the monastery for the "Oil of Gladness" preparation ceremony. The residue of the Myron, collected earlier, was now poured into three new cauldrons of olive oil, including oil from the Monastery of St. Mari Mina near Alexandria. His Holiness used a concordance to select various readings in Arabic, Coptic, and English. I was again invited to read, this time the story about Jacob's ladder in the Book of Genesis, as well as a passage from the Song of Songs which invokes the Spirit to come on this festive day.

Various bishops, as well as a missionary priest or two serving the Coptic Church abroad, were also asked to do some of the readings today. Other English speakers were asked to read: priests of the Coptic Church in the States and in Australia and a visiting bishop who is in union with the Orthodox Church of Egypt. Pope Shenouda also asked a visiting monk to read. He is a Catholic whom I have not met, who is just passing through for a few days. So this makes the second Catholic monk who has read and participated in the consecration of the holy oil during this week-long ceremony.

## Consecration of the Myron

APRIL 9, THURSDAY

Finally, the day has arrived to formally consecrate the Myron as well as the Ghalillion, that is, the Oil of Gladness. The vast crowd was barred from the sanctuary, for all the visiting prelates, monks, priests, nuns, and their families filled up the place. Dignitaries, the laity, and the curious had to remain outside the church, trying to hear the ceremony and even to observe it on the closed-circuit TV which had been brought in for the occasion. There were wires all over the place today.

Pope Shenouda asked me to do a reading from the Song of Songs during this ceremony—a ceremony which was made somewhat uncomfortable because of the great heat of the day. The last bit of the old Myron was mixed in with the new. This symbolic practice makes it theoretically possible that some of the old Myron from the Apostolic era is mingled in with the latest batch—an idea embodied in the Church's catechesis of worship as a sign of apostolic fidelity and continuity.

All the bishops and abbots in attendance were invited to participate, and there was great celebration, great joy in the air, following the concluding rites.

## The Rigors of Worship

APRIL 12, SUNDAY

It is Palm Sunday here. Masses, liturgies, and prayer services in general during this week will last twelve hours a day, minimally, and reach up to sixteen or eighteen hours a day by the Triduum! In addition to this, the monks practice a very strict bread-and-water fast during all of Holy Week, so it promises to be a rigorous religious exercise. Here is where the practice of the so-called "intensive-participant observation," the methodology of anthropologists, will prove to be most challenging for me. According to this method, I must follow, as much as humanly possible, the routine and the pattern of life of the people with whom I live. Otherwise, I shall never understand them as well as I should.

I keep reminding myself that, in a very real sense, God practiced intensive-participant observation by coming among us. In the season of Lent, we remember that he even participated in the ignominious fortunes of our common humanity. He shared the shame and the burden, the sorrow and the sin, even the death of our humanity so that, by offering his love in this manner, he might know us and we might know him more intimately than before.

## APRIL 15, WEDNESDAY OF HOLY WEEK

*Merciful Lord,*
*    The Cross, however wondrous and beauteous we conceive it, must remain the Cross you knew. What privilege, what intimacy of love it conceals. But it cannot change from what you yourself perceived it to be: the dreadful curse; the terrible baptism of pain; the poisonous cup of sorrows you would have prayed away. Were it ever otherwise, it would not be the Cross we received from you, the suffering of love we obediently accept in union with you. Help me to say "yes" again to the sign of your Cross over me!*

## APRIL 17, GOOD FRIDAY

There is hardly a moment of the day when we are not in church and, after a week of fasting on bread and water, most of us are rather wobbly on our feet. But I must say that living among a group of monks who are willing, even enthusiastic, to perform such ascetical works in the practice of their faith and their love of God makes the doing of it considerably easier than I thought it would be. In fact, very often, it seems to be a rather light thing, almost too light. Apparently what is done in the company of many brothers becomes much more doable than what one contemplates doing alone.

But if monks must swim against the current, if they must work against the grain, as sometimes it might seem in a monastery in America, then any ascetical works there seem to be both altogether too hard and, at the same time, inappropriate. In the West, asceticism is so often regarded as *passé*, or unhealthy and unwholesome. It is not appreciated, and those who practice it to any significant de-

gree at all are sometimes regarded as elitist, boastful, fundamental-
ist, or negative. It is refreshing to be in a place where no such complex agendas obtain. Here, fasting and mortifications of the body
are taken matter-of-factly. They are joyful, sacrificial gifts that are
offered to God in the company of one another, building a community out of the commonality of shared works and acts of faith.

### A Feast with a Future

APRIL 19, EASTER SUNDAY

The Easter Liturgy concluded this morning—the Vigil, that
is—at 3:00 A.M., and there was great feasting thereafter. I spoke to
Abuna Elia during the feasting and he said that "by the celebration
of Easter, the Church does not so much return in history to the
third day after the burial of Jesus, to the glorious moment when he
arose. It doesn't just return to the empty tomb with the apostles or
the disciples or Mary of Magdala. It does, indeed, do these things,
but it does these things in memory.

"On Easter Sunday," he said, "the Church is somehow trans-
ported to the future, when Christ will come again. Easter, for the
Church, is a promissory feast of one day fully sharing union with
Christ in a risen body. It's a celebration of the future when the
Church will be gathered around the Lamb in the new Jerusalem
with the heavenly assembly all around us, singing and praising
God. We believe that Christ will come again," he stated. "We believe in the second coming of Christ but, liturgically, we are already hastening that day; liturgically, we are already summoning
him. We are given a voice to call him forth, to bring him back by
our worship. The celebration of the Mass makes Christ present to
us Eucharistically. The Eucharistic coming of Christ," he concluded, "is of one fabric, one cloth, with the eschatological coming
of Christ on the last day."

Maybe it's all the fasting, all of the liturgical exercises, but I'm
inclined to hear the words of Abuna Elia with ready acceptance and
without any hesitation. Perhaps that is part of the benefit of a
Church that practices its liturgical and ascetical life as one life. It is,
therefore, able to express its spiritual and theological outlook with
pure zeal and great depth.

## A Rare Spring Holiday

APRIL 20, EASTER MONDAY

The Copts call this day "*shams el Nessim.*" It's an Egyptian spring holiday which falls on the Monday after Easter. The curious thing about this is that it's celebrated not only by the Christians, but by all sects. This is a uniquely Egyptian phenomenon, inasmuch as the majority of the population is Muslim, not Christian. Many are actually anti-Christian. They nevertheless celebrate a festive day of the Christian minority which is a movable feast calibrated on the liturgical calendar of the Coptic Church. So, ironically, the Moslems have to rely on the complex Coptic calendar to determine the date of their spring holiday!

I wonder at this, that the Moslems can permit themselves to celebrate a civil holiday in conjunction with the Christians' liturgical cycle. Surely the origin of this holiday must go back to a time when the numbers of Christians in Egypt closely approximated half or more of the population. Then, Christians and Moslems had cause to celebrate liturgical feasts and civil holidays together. As it is, I doubt that the Moslems would now be able to eradicate the holiday because it involves a day off from work. That is something which everyone of every religious stripe appreciates.

The pilgrims have come to the monastery in great numbers today. It is overflowing with people seeking to celebrate, not *shams el Nessim*, but Easter Monday. This is not only a spring holiday for the Copts; it's a day to travel, just as the two disciples traveled to Emmaus after the Resurrection. It's a day for the Copts to travel in the company of Christ to their beloved monasteries to enjoy a great feast. The monks are not hiding from the pilgrims today; they're not running away. Today they are sitting down with them at tables. All the monks, it seems, are content to immerse themselves in the company of the Copts who are visiting them. The joy of Easter briefly blurs the boundaries of separation between the urban laity and the desert monks.

APRIL 21, TUESDAY

Whatever else I was able to do today in terms of writing a letter or reading a book, it seems that I somehow spent most of the day in a very deep sleep. I think I was physically paying off all the debts that I have incurred over the last week in this monastery. But having been a lifelong insomniac, I only note that the sleep was better today than ever, perhaps a benefit of the Easter holiday. *The Lord gives to his beloved while they slumber* (Psalm 127:2).

## The Coptic Diaspora, Alas

APRIL 24, FRIDAY

Most of the clerics who were here for the consecration of the Sacred Myron departed before Holy Week, but two Coptic bishops from Europe have lingered. They are actually not native Egyptians at all; they are Europeans who by complex means have been enlisted in the service of the Egyptian Christian diaspora in Europe, especially in France. They speak English; actually, one of them speaks English quite well. So I had the opportunity to discuss the Coptic Church in diaspora with them.

Today, as we had lunch, I enjoyed hearing about their stories of the blessings of God on the Coptic Orthodox Church dispersed in Europe. But I also heard their pain. They lamented that so many of the young people who leave Egypt with good faith find themselves unable to negotiate the extraordinary secularity, materialism, and Gnosticism of the popular culture abroad. Almost because they are too innocent, too naive, they find themselves the objects of exploitation. One of the bishops told me that there must be a special tragic pleasure that the truly cynical and corrupt obtain from bringing a virtuous and innocent youth to folly.

It seems that the Copts have been singled out wherever they appear as a special target to make sure that, as much as possible, they should not only be exposed to the decadence of the culture around them but they should also be forced to participate in it. The bishops told me that, as priests of the Coptic Church in Europe, it is often their responsibility to "pick up the pieces." They must deal with the confusion of so many of the young Copts who have been deluded or deceived, who have been burdened with the guilt and the shame of what has happened in their lives since they left Egypt.

I can only imagine that what the bishops said is true enough. Unfortunately, it seems quite consistent with the kind of behavioral pattern I have observed in the States. But it grieves me to consider that the very same innocence and enthusiasm for all things religious and holy that have given me such delight since coming to Egypt, are likely to be for many others the cause of mischief and the source of ruin. Rather, would that we Westerners could come to realize that we have been missing great gifts, great wealth, great blessings. Would that we could observe the Copts among us and become, in a holy kind of jealousy, desiring to partake of the blessings which are theirs by birthright. How terrible, the unholy jealousy which requires us to rob them of their innocence so that neither they, nor we, can enjoy it! Instead, we have disdained it and make it impossible for them to retain it.

## APRIL 26, SUNDAY

*Gentle Shepherd,*

*You promised to rescue the lost lamb and search for the strayed sheep. Look tenderly upon your beloved children of this Church in Egypt. As gold in the furnace you have tested them, in the crucible of humiliation you have purified them. Suffering for your sake—estranged in their own land—you have ennobled them for the sacrifice of bearing witness. May the witness of their saints and the precious gifts of their martyrs who span their whole history be a prayer before you and a living sign they will always reverence.*

*By their prayer, save their children now in this dark time, and all who are scattered far from their homeland. Never let them forget the wealth of their heritage, nor neglect to honor your Cross so deeply anchored in their nation, their land, their memory, and their present pain. I thank you that you have given me a glimpse of their soul! How they shine in my eyes! Persuade me to still my soul anew amid all its previous concerns, and to rely upon your shepherd's love again.*

## Islamic Ramadan

### APRIL 29, WEDNESDAY

The monks told me that throughout Islamic Egypt, the Moslems have entered into the holy season of Ramadan, the time for their fasting and mortification. It is their equivalent of our Lent. The monks said that I must make some effort to leave the monastery during this season to observe the practice of the Moslems, and compare and contrast it with Coptic religious practice.

They told me that there is one important difference. The Moslem—that is, the practicing Moslem and many otherwise nominal ones—surely fasts from sunrise to sunset, not even drinking water during daylight hours in Ramadan. But, after sunset, quite the opposite occurs; it becomes a time of feasting! Indeed, the amount of food—delicacies as well as meats and grains in general and desserts of every kind—purchased in the shops in Egypt dramatically increases during the month of Ramadan. So it is a paradox of fasting and feasting simultaneously.

When Ramadan falls in the summer, when the days are longer, then the fasting is really difficult. To be without water in summer in Egypt is almost unbearable. So the amount of water which is drunk and the amount of food which is eaten after sunset in summer Ramadans can sometimes even lead to medical problems. Such an extraordinary pattern of behavior! Again, the monks insist that I should try to witness this phenomenon at closer range.

# MAY

## A TIME TO PRESS ONWARD

### *Oases and Graces*

MAY 1, FRIDAY

I met today with Abuna Elia who wanted to discuss with me again the meaning of the desert in the life of Jesus. We discussed how Christ had been driven into the desert by the Holy Spirit after his baptism in order to pursue the children of Adam and Eve who had been driven into the desert as a consequence of their sin (cf. Genesis 3:23-24). "That's why Jesus is the Good Shepherd who goes out into the desert waste to find the lost lamb and carry it back to the Father," said Abuna Elia. "That's why monks live in deserts, because they are following the same mystery. Love," he noted, "commissions us to follow after the loveless, to go to the places where they were lost."

According to Abuna Elia, the goat which was used for the Day of Atonement, the "scapegoat" upon which were laid the sins of Israel, was driven out to die in the desert at the conclusion of the rite. Similarly, Christ, upon whom the sins of the world were laid by love, was driven out into the desert by that same love so that in no dark place would we be absent from him, and in every place he would be present to us. Abuna Elia added, "The scapegoat was sent to suffer and die in the desert as a *sign*, but Jesus suffered and died on the Cross as the *reality* of our salvation. We are sent out into our own deserts in imitation of Christ in order to share in his saving work because love bids us to do so."

Then he pointed out that, "Whereas the goat was driven out into the desert *once*; for Christ, the desert would be an unrelenting mission. He still protests to Paul, after his Resurrection, that he suffers persecution! *'Saul, Saul, why do you persecute me?'* (Acts 9:4).

"So for us, in our weakness, in the fragility of our hearts and the inconstancy of our love, the desert had better have oases. There had better be respites for us, or we shall not survive. If we had had the strength and the focus, the centeredness of mind and heart to attain salvation of ourselves, we would hardly have required the work of a Savior. It was precisely *because* we lack these things that salvation was given to us as an undeserved gift and blessing. Therefore, when we are struggling to attain it, God kindly provides us with respite and relief in the oases of our lives."

Abuna Elia concluded our conversation today by observing that the dialogue we have been enjoying has been a respite for him because he has found in my attentive listening and my interest an opportunity for him to be refreshed, to be heard, to have someone respond to his thoughts in a way which he thought they warranted.

I reflected later how remarkable it is that a true desert father, nearing the end of his long life of solitude and asceticism, should speak so warmly and sympathetically about human frailty and weakness. How well he understands the need for the blessing of rests, of Sabbaths, yes, even of the gift of human presence, to punctuate what would sometimes seem to be the loveless lot of our human condition without God.

But it is not just faith in God which will sustain us. We also need the moments in which the presence of God is made perceptible, tangible, sacramental, or, as they would say in the East, "iconographic." Our faith is an interesting admixture of trusting God in the midst of emptiness and relying upon him for the gifts we need to continue the journey. May wisdom teach us how to wait on God's generous gifts of rest and refreshment, and not to indulge in desperate demands for them.

### Escape from Ramadan

MAY 3, SUNDAY

Temperatures have been rising here the last few days, sometimes climbing to over 100 degrees. The number of pilgrims is increasing now, not only because we are in the Easter season but also, in part, because they wish to escape the heat of the city and the commotion associated with the Islamic month of Ramadan. The festivities are loud and numerous in one apartment building after the other across the city. In the streets, likewise, the noise is great with the din of nightly celebrations. What an interesting "fasting season" is Ramadan!

## A Foiled Rat

MAY 6, WEDNESDAY

What with the heat becoming more oppressive, even at night, I've taken to spending longer and longer evenings in the church which is a little bit less oppressive than our cells.

During the summer nights, the church is lit by a number of oil lamps hanging from a wire suspended from the ceiling. These oil lamps are beautiful, rather antique. They burn their oil with a wick in a bottom pot. Between the pot of oil and the ceiling from which it hangs, suspended on that same wire, is an ostrich egg! I asked about the significance of the ostrich egg, why the monks hang it between the lamps and the ceiling, and the answers I received were rather diverse.

One monk told me that the ostrich is considered to be a fairly stupid bird and that if it did not continue to look at its eggs, it would forget where it had laid them. "Likewise," he said, "our soul is regarded in its fallen state of human sin to be somewhat dull and insensitive. We must keep our spiritual eyes fixed on God. We must gaze with eyes fixed on the truths of faith, as it were, fixed on the Cross. Otherwise, we shall forget from whom our life has come and the work for which we were commissioned. For that reason, the ostrich egg is placed above the oil lamp so it can always be seen. The glow of the lamp below casts light upon it." That sounded like a plausible symbolic account of the ostrich egg.

Another monk told me yet another variation of the story. He said that the ostrich has the capacity to warm the egg that it has laid, not so much by sitting upon it, but by gazing at it! It's one of those legends which have been preserved by ethnic folk for centuries. By gazing at the egg, the ostrich warms it until it comes to life, that is, until the baby bird breaks through the shell. In a similar way, the monk went on to say, "God keeps his gaze always resting gently on us. He summons us to life till we are ready to 'hatch,' as it were, to break through the limitations of this world into the kingdom of God in the world to come, to be born into eternity."

So, in this interpretation, the ostrich comes off in a much better light. Its egg is hung above the lamp to lay it bare to the gaze of God, just as we are always laid before the gaze of God, revealed to his sight. These and similar meditations I have kept in my mind throughout my months of living in this monastery when I look up at the oil lamps.

But last night I saw a scrawny desert rat crawling along a groove in the wall, creeping very slowly and with great stealth. It proceeded to slide down the wire till it came to the egg. However, when it tried to navigate the large, smooth surface, it couldn't get a grip. Its little claws had been so tightly closed around the wire that when it came to the egg, it couldn't open them wide enough to hold onto it. So it slipped off the egg and fell to the ground. The rat seemed to be injured by the fall. It scurried away in great discomfort, having failed to obtain the oil that it wished to drink from the lamp below. So it turns out that the eggs actually have a practical purpose. They keep the rats away from the lamps, away from the oil reserve which they might otherwise try to drink, desert rats being omnivorous.

How interesting that a little observation can reveal the hidden meanings of things, that the explanations that people give are often only part of the story. I don't question for a moment the symbolism attached to the ostrich eggs suspended over the oil lamps. But I believe there was a practical origin to this custom which then became elaborated into a variety of symbolic and spiritual interpretations thereafter. This may be just one example of many explanations given in religious and civil societies by which we try to account for the ways handed on to us, not so much in terms of the practical reasons for which they were started, but in terms of the symbolic interpretations which they later acquired.

### Blessings Grasped

MAY 9, SATURDAY

It seems to me that the number of pilgrims has been increasing throughout the Easter season. Today the church was crowded with them. Many of the monks who ordinarily mill about the monastery seem to be hiding. The pilgrims are beginning to oppress them. The "dispensation" of the Easter celebration has passed and the monks do not wish to be seen. They do not wish to be taxed by so many requests to converse, to pray, to confess, and to bless them. I

even saw monks trying to get away from pilgrims today by physically fleeing, raising their habits up to their knees, so that their legs
were freer to run. Nevertheless, two pilgrims took it on themselves
to run after the monks. Then was enacted before my eyes a formal
ritual of desert monastic life that I had read about, but had not actually seen till now.

In both cases, the monks did not run fast enough to out-dis-
tance the ones who were seeking their blessing. In both cases, each
pilgrim grabbed hold of the ankles of the monk he was pursuing,
and stopped him dead in his tracks. He obliged the monk to give a
blessing, or to say a word, or he would not let go! In both cases,
the monk seemed to accept this form of captivity as a necessary
component of his vocation in the desert. He turned around to his
captor, blessed him, and gave him a word or two of spiritual advice.
How wonderful this ritual, this formality, by which the monk
knows not to run too fast, by which the pursuer knows his efforts
will not be answered with curses or reproaches. Built into the feat
of capture is the grace of blessing and encouragement!

It seems to me that there are biblical parallels to this, such as
Jacob wrestling with the angel in the Book of Genesis. He strug-
gled with the angel all night and then, when the angel finally tried
to escape before dawn, Jacob said he wouldn't let him go unless he
received a blessing. So the angel blessed him and gave him the
name "Israel," thereby bestowing on him God's special favor.

### Debilitating Heat

MAY 12, TUESDAY

How heavy and slow I feel in this heat! All things take longer
to do. Every step seems to be slower; every thought, every idea
seems to proceed with greater gravity. I understand now, physically,
why people in tropical climates are regarded as more easy-going
than those in Nordic climes.

Afternoon activity in the monastery seems to have been suspended, and we are only in the middle of May. How it will be in
the middle of July or August I can only begin to imagine. But the
monastic liturgical routine continues as ever. I understand better
and better now why the greatest number of hours dedicated to
prayer are scheduled during the night. In the winter, it is too cold

to genuinely sleep at night. One needs to be moving, so standing and praying in the church is a way of coping with the extremity of the cold. Now, in the summer, one can't really sleep at night either; it's too hot. But being in the church is cooler than being in one's cell. In the chapel, at least, there is the social energy necessary to participate in the communal work of monastic prayer. So, the hours that are more bearable, more livable, both in winter and in summer, are dedicated to prayer in the middle of the night. In the summertime, this frees the hottest hours of the afternoon for relative inertia, as one is genuinely unable to physically work—or even think—effectively in the high temperatures.

I personally feel guilty for obsessing about the weather so much. I am just living my personal drama of a Sahara desert summer and what it means in *my* imagination, to *my* body. I should simply attempt to experience my surroundings in the spirit of those who live here year after year, rather than to project onto that experience what it means from my perspective. Besides that, in terms of my own spirituality and prayer life, my surrender to the present with all of its challenges, its blessings, as well as its hardships, is part of my embrace of the Paschal Mysteries. Not to exaggerate its burdens or its discomforts in order to make myself a victim in my own right, rather than one who shares in the blessing, the solidarity of the victimhood of Christ who is *the* victim, is my truest, most essential right of all.

MAY 14, THURSDAY

> *O Light of the World,*
> *I lit a candle today in the monastery church, and almost laughed at myself for the feeling that the pious gesture evoked in me. I dreaded adding the heat of a little flame to the already hot atmosphere! I did not want to contribute anything to the rising temperatures; my original purpose was to petition you for grace to bear it all better in these next few months.*
> *Would that I had such reluctance to add the slightest ill will by my words to the social atmosphere of uncharity in the world from which I came! And would that I begged for such divine protection from the deadly climate of cynicism and spite which afflicts the culture to which I will one day return.*

> *Nevertheless, I ask you to assist me to live here without complaining. If you do not relieve me of my discomfort, remind me always to offer it as prayer, and to accept it as a poor penance for my failures in growing up into the maturity, the eternal childhood, of your love. May the heat remind me of those things that I should truly dread above physical pain. Purify me for a life of greater holiness and charity.*
>
> *And please, don't let my candle add one degree to the warmth of this place!*

## The Insistence of the Sisters

MAY 16, SATURDAY

Another day of pilgrims, another day of the soliciting of blessings. There are so many pilgrims now that some of the monks have seemingly thrown me out to them. The monks direct the pilgrims to me so that there are fewer pilgrims oppressing them.

This afternoon while I was in the church, three older sisters from a poor family in Beni Suef in Upper Egypt came to seek a blessing from me. I could hardly understood their dialect, and I think they could hardly understand me. I thought that the two sisters on either side of the middle one were asking me to advise her to pay better attention to them, to listen to them more thoughtfully. I thought they were saying in Arabic that they wanted me to make their sister listen, to make their sister hear. So I tried to speak to the sister in the middle. I tried to convince her to be more open, more receptive, more attentive to her sisters on either side of her.

The two sisters on either side heard what I was saying and looked vexed. "No, no, Abuna," they said, "that's not what we mean." So I stated my case more firmly to the sister in the middle. I told her it was her Christian obligation and her responsibility from baptism to be hospitable to the members of her family, to show the person of Christ in his patience and forbearance to them. The sisters on either side looked even more disturbed than before. "No, no, Abuna, that's not what we mean."

Then I looked helplessly at both of them, gesturing that I could not understand them at all. I threw both my hands in the air, palms face up, to show my lack of comprehension. When I did that, each sister grabbed one of my hands. They placed them over the right and left ears of the sister in the middle. Then I understood what they meant. Their sister was losing her hearing. She was virtually deaf, and they wanted me to give her a blessing, to pray for the restoration of her hearing. So what else could I do but to pray, inasmuch as both of my hands were being held over the ears of the sister in the middle? I prayed, then, almost in spite of myself, more amused by the sisters' originality and cleverness in obtaining the blessing they desired than by the gravity of their request.

I finally removed my hands and thought more than anything about how I was going to make my escape from these imposing women. As they walked away, I began to bless a few other people. But, in a matter of a few minutes, I heard them making the ululations, the sound that Arabic women make when they are filled with joy. I heard the tongue-rolling cries of excitement that rippled forth from their mouths.

The two women were now crying out to everyone in the middle of the church that their sister could hear—that she who had been deaf was now able to hear them and to understand the words they were speaking to her! At that, everyone began to applaud, to sing, to praise God, or to ululate. I was taken aback by the din, and used it as a smoke screen for quickly making my escape. I was almost afraid that the excitement that had been generated would make the monks an even greater object of pursuit by those who are so anxiously seeking blessings.

I do not know, now, upon reflection, what really transpired with the three sisters. I don't know if the one had been actually deaf and her hearing was now restored, or if she had been partly deaf and thought her hearing was somewhat improved. I don't know if she actually heard her sisters better, or if in their excitement they were speaking louder than before. I don't know if, in their mutual desire to receive this blessing, they were more responsive, more receptive to every kind of signal that they were communicating to each other. I don't know if they so highly desired to experience the catharsis of a healing that they were able to turn this disability into an occasion of grace.

I don't know. But I do know that God was there, and that they were receptive to his presence and power. They knew how to take this occasion of seeking and desiring and praying and find in it a joyful experience of God's healing. I'm content with that. Miracles may happen, but even if this was not a miracle, it is a grand miracle of grace that people can enfold such occasions as these into the economy of salvation, that they can experience them in the limitations and the fragilities of our human lives as genuine, divine visitations of power and love.

## *A Wrenching Transition*

MAY 17, SUNDAY

After the Kodes in St. Bishoi Church today, I was greeted by my friends from Cairo who had come to the monastery to escort me back to the city. They knew that my months of living in Deir Anba Bishoi must surely come to a close now if I am to make any kind of visit to the other monasteries of Egypt. So I had a kind of farewell. I told the monks that I would probably be coming back here on several more occasions as I make my circuit of the other monasteries. I'm sure that is true, so the farewell was made somewhat easier. And yet this is the end of the longest stay of my research year, and I have grown so much at home and so much at ease here, so familiar with this setting, so at one with the monks in their prayer and so appreciative and admiring of their faith that I feel very sad at departing from them. But my research has always been circumscribed by limitations of time. I have always been aware of this, so I am moving on with a degree of genuine resignation.

Coming back to Cairo was jarring. The city is bustling at this time of the year. Even with the heat as high and oppressive as it is, it's still a very busy and noisy city. Now that I have come back in the middle of the month of Ramadan, it seems even louder and noisier than ever. The loudspeakers on the minarets are turned up very high, so the call to prayer at night as well as throughout the day is much louder than before. All night long, the Islamic neighbors in the apartment building in which I'm staying are celebrating their seasonal feast just as emphatically as they celebrate the daily fast. The noise and the sound of partying and family conviviality is as intrusive and invasive as the call to prayer from the minarets. A Jew at Christmas, a Copt at Ramadan.

So I will not stay long in Cairo. I will take advantage of the earliest possible rides I can procure to visit the other monasteries. Actually, I am committed to doing so in order to complete my research year and the rest of my fieldwork.

MAY 20, WEDNESDAY

> *Provident God,*
> *It was never mine, O God. I knew it then and acknowledge it now: the monastery with its hallowed chants and hooded monks; the enclosed desert fortress with its parapets and towers, its vine arbors and orange orchards; the incense-saturated church of St. Bishoi's pilgrims and its icons of silent, interceding apostles. They are all yours. From you I received them as my life's most unlikely gift, and from them I make my departure, grateful for what I have gained from them. Even in the sign of their eventual loss, I remain grateful for what can never now be taken from me. I go now to other monasteries in other provinces of your eternal desert. But all of them are yours, and since they are yours, I shall become richer still for remaining in you, and poorer by my ever departing from them!*

## Little Forays All About

MAY 21, THURSDAY

I've been in Cairo this week, making plans for the next and last two months of my Egyptian sojourn. Emil Kamal-Hanna has insisted on providing me with the assistance of three college students: Nasser, Tarek, and Ihab. They are to carry my bags; they are to do errands for me and to assist in rapid dialoguing in Arabic whenever I am in need of its more refined or subtle usages. They are to be my companions and to attend to all my needs along the way. I'm really quite overwhelmed by the generosity of the Copts in this respect. I'm certain that this is all being arranged with no expectation of payment. Indeed, there would be a refusal were I to suggest payment. The students are simply delighted to have the opportunity to accompany a foreigner, an American monk, and to be able to dialogue with me along the way. I'm sure that I could manage on my own, and I'm a little bit disappointed not to have the opportunity to try to do so. But I have been so warmly welcomed by the Coptic community here and they are absolutely determined to provide every kind of accommodation for me. "If a monk is a welcomed guest of the desert monks, he should travel with Copts in attendance at all times in the city," Emil assures me.

I'm staying at the house of the Kamal-Hannas in Heliopolis, enjoying a few days of feasting. Madame Juliet, the matron of the house, is extremely hospitable and treats every day in which a guest lives in her home as a day of celebration, a day of great generosity. I'm gaining weight, I think, from just a few days of being here. Italian Sunday dinners have nothing on the hospitality of the daily fare here!

## MAY 25, MONDAY

*O God Who Is,*

*I miss you! You are with me in this place; your eye is on me and your hand is over me, but I cannot find you in the city as I remember you in the desert. How wonderful and how strange! When I lived there these past few months, I thought that you were so transcendent, so totally other. You were the God who lived infinitely above the arid earth. But I must have been swimming in the pool of your presence there, and did not know it then. Only now do I realize it in the loss, and I feel every bit the "fish out of water," as the Desert Fathers described the monk fallen back upon the habitation of men.*

*"Holy ground," you told Moses, "requires shoes to be removed." How I delight to take off my shoes as do the Copts when they enter their churches. But I delighted no less to walk barefoot on desert floors, understanding at last that the transcendence of your nature has its reflected image in mine. Nowhere am I more at home than in the otherness of your holy ground. We remove our shoes upon coming home as a humble sign that we live in this world as your servants. Help me to serve you in my loss of the home I had with you, and to accept my commerce with all these people as a means of drawing near to you again as you hide in them.*

# JUNE
## A TIME TO VISIT NEW PLACES

### *Deir el Baramous*

JUNE 1, MONDAY

We rented a jeep today and drove to the Monastery of el Baramous, that is, the Monastery of the Romans. It is also situated in
the desert of the Wadi Natroun, not very far from St. Bishoi, but it
is one of the monasteries I have visited least often during my stay
so far. Deir el Baramous was ostensibly founded by two Roman
brothers who came here in admiration of the Egyptian monastic
enterprise, and stayed. They are regarded as brothers of high birth.
They surrendered everything and lived an exemplary monastic life
centuries and centuries ago. The monastery, like all the others in
the region, is relatively young in terms of the age of its members
and is rapidly expanding. I'm impressed by the archaeological interests of some of the monks who are doing very careful, painstak-
ing excavations and reconstructions of some of the oldest sites, especially in the old church here.

JUNE 3, WEDNESDAY

I've had some opportunity to study the liturgy, the psalmody of
the Coptic Church, a little bit more intently while I'm here. The
monks are very careful about its execution in this monastery and
are able to speak at greater length about its rationale and its aesthetic purposes. So I'm trying to enter more deeply into the
monastic prayer here, especially in the grace of my reprieve of departing Cairo and returning to the sanctuary of a desert monastery.

## The Cave of a Saint

JUNE 5, FRIDAY

I've been given the opportunity to spend a few days and nights in a cave within walking distance from the monastery. It was once the eremitical preserve of the monk called "Abuna Mina el Muttawahad, the Solitary," who later became Pope Kyrillos VI. The cave of this beloved pope of the 1960s—much regarded as a saint by the Copts—has become a pilgrimage site. It is not a good place for me to stay much by day, since there are many visitors. It's a lovely place, this rock niche, in which to rest and to enjoy the desert silence and the desert sky which I can see out beyond the opening. Is it the sainted Solitary who whispers to me from heaven in the night breezes of the Sahara?

## The Monastery of Olive Groves

JUNE 10, WEDNESDAY

Nasser, Tarek, Ihab, and I continued farther north on our travels to the Monastery of Mari Mina which has been completely reconstructed. It was named after St. Mina who had a large following in Egypt over a thousand years ago. He is regarded as a mystic and a great saint with the gift of healing. There's been a revival of interest in St. Mina, and people are coming to this monastery to seek blessings from the intercession of their beloved patron.

This monastery has a beautiful orchard of olive trees which is a site for the production of olive oil. Much of the oil used in the Sacred Myron and the ceremony of its blessing came from these trees. The desert sand around the monastery is littered with little green shards or glass splinters, which the monks tell me are the residue of the old vessels in which the oil of St. Mina was once stored. That is to say, people came here to obtain oil from the ancient olive groves a thousand years ago; the oil was used for the blessing of the sick. The number of pilgrims was so great and the number of glass vessels so numerous that even the accidental breakage of a few of them, here and there, littered the desert floor over the course of time with many signs of this past and popular devotion.

*The author praying in the shallow cave of Pope St. Kyrillos VI.*

The abbot of the monastery reminded me that the Garden of Gethsemane was an olive garden. Indeed, the Hebrew name "Gethsemane" implies the place of an olive oil press. The abbot declared that the growing of olive trees and the production of oil is appropriate for this monastery, because the monastic life has, as one of its iconographic meanings, "living in union with Jesus in his moment of prayer." He said, in effect:

> "We heard Jesus using the very intimate and personal word 'Abba' to call upon God. We heard it most profoundly during his prayer in the Garden of Gethsemane. So monks, in union with Christ, are able to pray this most profound, intimate discourse with God frequently only when they are open and available to suffering. According to the mercy of God and the mission of Christ, suffering as an intercessory act of prayer is a sign of love and a gesture of trust in God's will and Providence."

I can't help but remember that Thomas Merton's monastery in the States is called "Gethsemani."


JUNE 12, FRIDAY

We returned to Cairo today and are planning for a little venture tomorrow to Port Said. Emil Kamal-Hanna is a friend of the bishop of this diocese, and he wishes me to speak with him at length about Coptic ecclesiastical life at this time.


### Oriented and Disoriented Prayer

JUNE 13, SATURDAY

We took a ride through the desert north of Cairo in the direction of Port Said and passed the most beautiful sand dunes I have ever seen. I had once thought that the desert of the Sahara was comprised largely of sand dunes but, when I was preparing for my fieldwork here and read about the topography of the desert, I was saddened to discover that it is mostly gravel. There are only a few areas that are covered with sand dunes, but we finally passed through a sizable one today, and it was most impressive.

Port Said is a functional, mercantile city—not what I would have thought to be a tourist town. The bishop is a very bright and articulate man with a vision for the Church in this region. He informed me that the number of Copts who live in this sector of Egypt is somewhat less than the national average. In some parts there are fairly empty corridors, but in the city itself, because of trade, there is a higher pluralism of peoples and a greater number of Christians. These Christians are of many kinds, especially aging populations of Italian Catholics and the Orthodox of Eastern Europe, as well as a significant number of younger Copts. The non-Copts, though, have been steadily moving out of the area, as industry and trade are progressively becoming more and more nationalized. The bishop said that the loss of the non-Coptic Christians has somewhat weakened the Christian presence in the region.

The Copts are keen on purchasing churches, especially Catholic churches, which have been abandoned by the receding populations. In fact, the Coptic cathedral in this city is actually a converted Catholic church. The interesting thing about it is that the church—which is not such an old one, after all—was not built on the traditional east-west axis on which classical Catholic churches were formerly built. So when the bishop adapted it for Coptic use, he put the sanctuary and the pews on an east-west axis, even though the building space itself doesn't quite accommodate this arrangement. It's odd to see a church in which the pews are placed up and down the length of the nave. The altar in the sanctuary is in a transept where I would expect a side niche of the church to be. But it works.

The Copts are determined to maintain the traditional orientation of prayer, that is, facing east, facing the rising sun. They consider the rising sun to be a sign of the Resurrection of Christ Jesus, a sign of Easter. Of course, above all people, the Copts are determined to preserve the natural sign value of the sun in terms of its Christian iconography, because their ancestors, before they became Christians, were worshipers of the sun. The Copts never forget the utility of the sun as a Christian sign and symbol.

It does make me pause and reconsider the loss of this orientation in Western architecture. We still require a sun, no less than the Copts do, but we do not see its symbolic significance as much as these desert dwellers do. It seems to me that the recent loss of architectural orientation toward the sun deprives modern church

*The gate of St. Anthony Monastery.*

architecture of a fuller religious significance. I believe that architectural disorientation is simultaneously both the cause and the result of the spiritual, moral disorientation of the Western religious world. I fear that our churches are more often "oriented" toward efficient parking lots, rather than to symbolic, spiritual centers.

## St. Anthony and Monasticism

JUNE 15, MONDAY

We traveled north again on the way toward Cairo, but instead of continuing in that direction, we turned into the Eastern Desert. We arrived at length this afternoon at the Monastery of St. Anthony.

St. Anthony is regarded as the founder of Egyptian monasticism, and is quite possibly the founder of all Christian monasticism. Like St. Francis many, many centuries later, he heard the Gospel account of the rich young man who was asked by Jesus to give up everything that he possessed to follow him. However, when Anthony learned about the tragedy of that young man's refusal to accept Christ's invitation, he was given the grace to generously and enthusiastically follow the Lord. In all probability, St. Anthony lived in a number of locations, but the monastery named after him is now regarded as the primary locus of his desert mission and his monastic vision.

There is a cave on the rather stark and high mountain ridge above the monastery where St. Anthony is said to have lived for considerable parts of his life. The monks assured me that I should be able to spend some time at prayer in that cave. I hope so.

## The Elusive Sowha

JUNE 16, TUESDAY

I spoke to one relatively young monk about a group of monks who are said to live in this area of the desert. They do not live in cells of a monastery, nor within the walls of a monastery, nor do they even live in caves. These monks are said to simply dwell out-of-doors, fulfilling the biblical role that Jesus once spoke of when he said, *"The bird has its nest and the fox has its lair, but the Son of Man has no place to lay his head"* (Matthew 8:20). This homelessness of Jesus, by which he was thrown outside the walls of the city, sacrificed outside the camp in the traditional biblical sense, has become a vocational type for this special class of monks. They comprise a very small number, to be sure, but they have a monastic identity for which I know of no Western counterpart. These are the *sowha* or "pilgrim monks" I discussed with Abuna Tadros earlier in January.

The young monk told me that we would take a walk later in the week while I am here and perhaps at night we might hear their chants. Sometimes these monks can be heard singing their psalmody in the canyons of the desert mountains around the monastery. The monk said that some people believe that if you should actually see a *sowha*, or speak with one, it would be a sign that God was about to call you home.

Ordinarily, people have no contact whatever with the *sowha*. These monks make their life from what they can glean from the desert floor. No food is provided for them; there is no special provisioning of water and certainly no other attentions medically or socially. They are at one with the environment—not just in some spiritual way, but actually, through the sheer vigor of faith and grace within their bodies and souls. The desert has become their paradise!

The young monk told me that these men are closer to heaven than to earth. If they should die in the desert, their passage out of this world to heaven would be a short one, since they had already made the greatest journey in their bodies before they died. By grace, they might be permitted to return along the way they had come. That is, if God should want to send them on a mission, or if he should want to hear his praises rise up again from the desert floor, he might send them back. So, every now and again, the monk said, it happens that the departed *sowha* may come into the monastery church at night and conduct religious services before the time of morning prayer. Even those who are long gone from this earth, the monk told me, are sometimes allowed to return to offer their prayers and praise to God for his glory.

I have no idea how to regard the historicity of such claims as these. But it is a powerful incentive to consider that there are those so blessed and so close to God in this world that their passage from it is a short one. For the rest of us, however, it is the greatest possible passage, well beyond our imagining.

## *Of Mountain Tops and Hermits' Caves*

JUNE 19, FRIDAY

I have now been privileged to spend a day and a night on the mountain of St. Anthony. The path to the cave is rather a rigorous one to ascend: rocky and slippery, actually a little dangerous here and there. All the more enthusiastically did I find myself climbing to the mountain top. Staying in the cave was an extraordinary joy. The silence was indescribable, and the view from the top of the mountain was also unimaginable. Even the Red Sea could be seen far, far on the eastern horizon. I even thought that I could see almost as far as Cairo from the mountain top.

Perched atop this mountain, so far from the world below, yet visually so close to much of it—perhaps it was because he could live here that Anthony would sometimes be compelled by grace to go down the mountain. He would travel to those places that he could see in the distance to proclaim the message of God's prophetic will and God's judgment and God's plan to believers who had grown negligent of his truth or his law. To be both in solitary prayer and yet visually cognizant of the needs of the world is the foundation of a dynamic apostolate. The Gospel recalls that Jesus observed his apostles in danger as they were crossing the sea while he was on the mountain in prayer. This must be emblematic!

It occurs to me that I am collecting in my memories a number of caves in which I have been privileged to pray. All the way back in the Wadi Natroun, I was sometimes able to pray in the cave near St. Bishoi Monastery. I remember how the abbot directed me to tie the wire that hung from the ceiling of that cave around my hair or my beard so that I would remain standing and not sit down or drift off into sleep during the time of my retreat. I also remember the cave of Pope Kyrillos near the Monastery of el Baramous. Now I have come to the cave of St. Anthony in the desert, the very cave in which I am given to believe that the original impulse for the monastic life—and, therefore, my own monastic life—was born. In a certain sense, the religion of Israel was born in a cave when God gave the Law to Moses on Mount Sinai. Even our own Christian faith was born in a cave, the cave of Bethlehem.

### *"Fountains and Springs, Bless the Lord"*

JUNE 20, SATURDAY

We traveled today to the relatively smaller Monastery of St. Paul, only a few miles from the Monastery of St. Anthony. It has a constantly running spring, although it is not so plentiful a water source as the spring at St. Anthony's. The monks in both of these monasteries claim that angels directed their founders to these springs and that they flow in whatever abundance is necessary to provide for the needs of those who live here—less water when less is necessary, and more water when more is necessary, according to God's generosity. How sweet, how profound to believe that the world is regarded as generous according to the measure of God's own generosity! The monks assume that they were brought to these sites of watery abundance because it was God's good and gracious will that they be directed here.

I could, I suppose, be more clinical—not to say "cynical"—about the manner by which the monks arrived in these places. There were, after all, centuries of nomads in the area before they arrived; there were Bedouins who would have known where springs existed. As noted earlier, the monks themselves have been here for centuries, and could have easily determined the best locations in which to build their monasteries. It didn't necessarily require divine guidance. I can see this as a process of selection over time, rather than miraculous intervention.

It reminds me so much of the kinds of problems I must cope with when people are always asking me about creation versus evolution. Creationist people like to think it was a miraculous intervention of God by which the species "man" came to be, whereas evolutionists like to see creation as a process of selection, slowly unfolding over time. Like many, I do not see that there is necessarily any conflict between God's will unfolding slowly versus God's will unfolding quickly. Slowness in the unfolding of God's will does not deprive the process of the miraculous, nor does swiftness in the unfolding of his will guarantee it. God is God. The world is his, and the processes by which his will is accomplished are regarded as either blessed or not, miraculous or not, depending upon whether or not one has eyes to see and ears to hear, depending upon whether or not one has received the grace to understand. Angels led the monks to these fountains, no less than if Bedouins directed them. The circumstances by which the monks were brought here should not be reduced to their logistical travel plans or geological surveys.

## Egypt's Oldest Monastery

JUNE 22, MONDAY

We now traveled across the Suez Canal to the Sinai peninsula and made our way south to a desert highway and through the craggy hills toward the Monastery of St. Catherine. At some distance from the monastery, we parked our jeep and walked up the hill. We arrived after the sun had set and saw the monastery against the mountain base—a jewel in the starlight.

The guest master let us in, gave us a room, and told me that perhaps the abbot would see me tomorrow.

JUNE 23, TUESDAY

The abbot was not so congenial in seeing me this time as he had been before, when I stopped here briefly on my return from Israel. This monastery is not Coptic; it is Greek Orthodox, and I am variously reminded that these monks are somewhat significantly less ecumenical than are the Coptic Orthodox. Whatever the theological outlook of the higher clergy of the two Churches, the Coptic Orthodox are by nature more congenial in their personal interrelations with Catholic monks and priests, or even laity. The Greek Orthodox, by contrast, express their disapproval of the Western Church by exhibiting that displeasure one-on-one to its members. The intensity with which some of them do so is so flagrant that I expect they partly validate the "rightness" of their claims to orthodoxy by the uncompromising displays of their disdain for us "heterodox" Romans. Ethnocentrism meets orthocentrism.

## Of Manna in the Wilderness

JUNE 24, WEDNESDAY — A Postscript

Wanting to explore the area round about the monastery and not wishing to prevail too much upon the thin hospitality of the monks here, I decided to drive the jeep myself to a site which I had been told was not too many miles away. There are copper mines here, supposedly once utilized by the Pharaohs of Egypt thousands of years ago. In these copper mines, I am told, have been found signs of the ancient Egyptian religion, signs of the devotion of the miners or their taskmasters. These include, among other things, small calf or cow-like statues reminiscent of the story of the sacred cow fashioned by the Hebrews at the base of Mount Sinai, this very mountain at which I am now staying. So I drove in the direction of the mines, having been given good directions, only to discover that the jeep was not in perfect working order. After some problems in negotiating the difficult terrain, the engine died.

I was in a rather precarious situation, reminiscent of the movies in which you see a poor soul dragging himself across the desert sand under the hot Sahara sun, desperate for water. Well, I wasn't quite so desperate, but, in my imagination, I was playing out every such movie scene I had ever seen.

I walked quite a distance looking for some help or a resting place in the shade when, finally, I noticed a goat. I realized that there are no wild goats in this desert and that it must belong to an encampment of some kind. So, without disturbing it, I followed the animal from a distance until it led me to the tents of its owner in an encampment of Bedouins of the tribe of Muzeina. I noted that the tents were made of black goat hair, constructed on palm tree poles. Bedouins normally live near mountain sides where *bir* (springs) can be found, or travel to *uaha* (oases) for water to make their bread.

I presented myself at the first tent, where the father of the dwelling, burly and larger than life, lavishly welcomed me in the custom so typical of the Arab world. He sat me down on pillows and, with the precious water of his house, washed my feet and my hands and gave me to drink. His children went out to gather a variety of delicacies from the neighboring tents, and his wife prepared a gracious meal for me. No doubt about it, I was an item of interest!

Part of the reason for this hospitality is that people who live in the desert seldom find strangers to entertain, so, when they do, it is an occasion for them to be able to receive someone generously, even excessively. It is also a mark of nobility in their society to be extravagant with their guests. And finally, it's a kind of safety net for them. They try to make the desert a place of hospitality rather than one of fear, for it might happen that any of them, at various times in their lives, could find themselves lost and alone there, and in need of welcome and assistance.

So, according to the norms of their culture, I was received with great kindness. Part of the hospitality of the father of the tent-dwellers was to pour out at my feet the equivalent of a bushel of cakes of bread!

It's marvelous how the nomads in this region bake their bread. Since water is scarce in the desert, they must do all of their baking during those relatively few times when they are close to a generous supply of water. They make a lot of bread and carry it with them as they travel. To prevent it from becoming stale on the journey, they bake their bread with a thick, hermetically sealed crust, which keeps the inside moist and fresh. Once a cake of bread is opened, it must be eaten more or less all at once, because it cannot be saved. No plastic wrap, no tinfoil, no tupperware here. Their means of preservation is a thick crust in its integrity. Once broken, all the contents must be eaten or they will be lost.

The father of the tent-dwellers picked up one of the cakes of bread at my feet and broke it open for me. I scooped out the insides and ate the delicious bread. Even as I was eating the first cake, he broke another and put it before me. I thanked him and said that I had had enough now, but he urged me to a third one, even though I was only nibbling at the second. I told him that I was really satiated, and that I would need to leave soon. Could he help me get back to the jeep, or could he take me to the monastery? I couldn't linger much longer; I was expected somewhere else. He broke the third cake, and urged me to have a fourth!

I have sometimes been in the home of a Mediterranean family, an Italian house, for a Sunday dinner and know the impossibility of saying "no." Somehow the gift of food is linked in an inextricable way with the gift of self. To reject the food is to somehow reject the giver of the food, and to consume the food is to offer the gift-giver the greatest affirmation. Here I found myself exactly in such a situation. I was forcing myself to eat a third cake and to nibble at a fourth. And even then my host began to urge me heartily to a fifth, and a sixth, and a seventh!

When my protests became louder and more forceful, the head of the house did something really incredible! He took one cake after the other from all that were lying before me—all of the bread of his family—and broke each one open, in front of my face! The gesture was unmistakable. He wanted me to know that he had withheld from me *nothing,* that he had put before me everything at his disposal. He wanted me to know that I had been well received, and by this gesture, this extravagant waste, this complete sacrifice, I would be persuaded, convinced, of his kindness. I would be certain of his hospitality.

I learned that the camp possessed a jeep of its own, in fact, hidden in a back tent. That evening, my host and his family drove me back to my abandoned jeep, which turned out to be in better shape after it had cooled down. After tinkering with it briefly, they followed me back to St. Catherine Monastery and kissed me good-bye.

It occurs to me now just how important breaking bread really is in the Near East, what a significant sign it is. Breaking bread is a gesture whose significance in the Mass, Coptic or Catholic, is fully resonant with the Bedouin mentality. It is reminiscent of the desert custom of the nomads who still live on the mountain on which Moses was told by God that the children of Israel would receive bread from heaven. God was, as it were, breaking bread with Israel, just as Christ broke bread with his apostles. I realize better that, like my Bedouin host, nothing has been kept back from us by God. Nothing has been withheld, and all has been generously supplied. The juxtaposition of Eucharistic bread-breaking and Paschal self-giving is a strong illustration of divine self-emptying love.

## June 26, Friday

*O God of Israel,*

*Here, you were a pillar of fire and a column of smoke. Here, the holy ground trembled, and Moses, your barefoot servant, spoke to you "face to face, as a friend speaks to his friend." You gave the Israelites the Torah, and they were never the same. The word you gave them in a howling wilderness was far more secure a home for them than the Promised Land to which they were traveling. The land was, after all, taken from them again and again, but your Word took up a dwelling at last so sure in them that one daughter of Zion bore It flesh and blood to the world. Maybe the Promised Land was always meant to be your word, but till that Word became man, mere men could only account it a word which deeded over your second-best gift and the bitter-sweet sign of your Providence: the Land of Israel.*

*Moses must have learned that the human heart itself is the very best repository of your word and promise; that the heart in dialogue with you is the holy ground, the most Promised Land, and the most solemn place of your rest. Moses never entered Israel; his body and his burial place are hidden. He, like Elijah, was taken up into the mystery of your dialogue with him. Moses and Elijah both came to "this mountain," the mount of intimacy with you.*

*They both came to Jesus on Tabor before he carried the whole weight of our tragic race into a sacred discourse with you on Calvary. The dialogue of the Father and the Son: therein is the cloud which came down on Sinai; therein is the light reflected on the face of Moses. Please accept my prayers here as a willing, silent attention to their heavenly converse which I cannot hear in so many words, but which I may at length repeat to others in holy, human commerce if I love them.*

# ✺ JULY
## A TIME FOR FAREWELLS

### *The Crucible of Upper Egypt*

JULY 1–3, WEDNESDAY–FRIDAY

The last several days have been spent taking a train tour of
Egypt, south of Cairo, traveling from one village to the next into
areas of Egypt that are more and more Coptic. As we pass through
towns that are increasingly Christian, there is a noticeable change in
the landscape. The number of church steeples with crosses atop
them begins to show as high a frequency as the number of minarets
with crescent moons on top. The skyline is sometimes dramatic because of this—and strangely beautiful. If only the faithful of both
religions could so beautifully coexist as their towers on the horizon!

The tensions between the Christians and the Moslems in this
area are greater than in the north. Perhaps it is because the Christians have a higher profile here; perhaps they are more outspoken
here. Perhaps just the very sign of them atop the churches, as well
as their greater numbers, confirms the success they enjoy. This
makes the lack of unanimity, the fact that the nation is not entirely
Islamic, more difficult for the Egyptian majority to endure. A number of Moslems have recently told me how painful it is for them to
acknowledge that, after so many centuries, there are still people in
Egypt who are not Muslim. They say that since it is obvious to
anyone with an open mind that Mohammed is God's prophet, it is
difficult, even agonizing, from their perspective, to imagine that so
many cannot grasp this "truth." They wonder if it is, indeed, hard-
headedness, hard-heartedness, contempt, or arrogance, by which
the Copts refuse the "obvious truth" of the Islamic religion.

I somehow sympathize with the Moslems on one level. Why should one hold to a religion he does not think is true, and why shouldn't it be true for everyone if it is true for him? But I also sympathize with the Copts, of course, and I sympathize more and more with the Jews throughout the ages. They must have always been in a position analogous to that of the Copts of Egypt.

I met the aging bishop of Beni Suef, Anba Athanasius. He is very kind. He gave me a tour of the church and the grounds immediately around his chancery and has instructed some of his servants to be hospitable to me while I am in his diocese.

### Coptic Deaconesses

I have met many "deaconesses," the equivalent of the apostolic religious sisters we know in the West. But since the Copts think of religious women in terms of the contemplative, eremitical life of the "Mothers" behind an enclosure, they do not call these women "Sister." Rather, they refer to them as "deaconesses" because of their work in the Church of serving the poor and the young, as well as a variety of other charities. They are not ordained deaconesses in the ordinary meaning of the word "ordination" to us. This reference is a problem for us, I told them, because the ordination of women as deacons is a matter of debate in the Western Church. They're simply innocent altogether of the idea that women might aspire to the prerogatives of office which are associated with the manhood of Christ and his apostles. So they can use the word "deaconess" and yet not associate it at all with the word "deacon" when that word is linked with ordination to the priesthood or with Holy Orders.

These women, by and large, are young, healthy, strong, and numerous. There's a growing movement of apostolic religious life for women in Egypt. I should one day like to study this phenomenon here. The very kind of life which is dying out in my country has caught on in Egypt and is proving to be a great boon to the life of the Coptic Church. These deaconesses wear habits of a modified sort—that is to say, we in the West would recognize them as Religious but their habits do not impede their apostolic service as Western Sisters often allege. In some ways, there is an interesting aesthetic symmetry between the "religious deaconesses," as they are known in Egypt, and the growing number of Islamic women who are wearing traditional Islamic garments by which their heads are veiled.

## Of Weavers and Rug-Makers

JULY 4, SATURDAY

In the outskirts of Beni Suef I came to a village that was entirely Coptic. I was given a tour of the church in that town, and I visited some of the homes and shops. In one of the shops I stood watching a number of rug-makers at their trade. They sped a shuttle back and forth on a Coptic loom, built like those that were used in Pharaonic times. It was fascinating; it was amazing.

I said to one of the rug-makers, "What if you make a mistake with the shuttle? You are going so fast that you will not see the error in the design until you have woven several layers over it. What will you do then? Will you unwind the carpet and remove the layers of thread that you have added?"

"No," said the rug-maker, "we would never do that; that would take far too much time. I'll tell you a secret. The most beautiful rugs with the most elaborate designs, the most expensive weavings, are the ones with mistakes hidden inside."

"How's that?" I asked. "Well, once we notice the mistake, we have to integrate it into the pattern. We have to change the pattern to include the mistake and make it part of a new design. Sometimes the new design is far more complex, far more embellished than anything we could have created ourselves. That's why the most beautiful rugs are the ones with mistakes hidden deep inside."

A great deal of wisdom in this Oriental art! Perhaps it's like the Providence of God, for sometimes the people with the deepest wounds or the most serious flaws exhibit the greatest glory of human nature.

## The Mulid of Deir el Muharraq

JULY 5, SUNDAY

I arrived at the Monastery of el Muharraq today. Deir el Muharraq is the only monastery in Egypt which is not situated entirely in the desert, although in order to maintain the idiom of desert existence, one face of it abuts the desert. It is a monastery in a much more traditional European sense, one around which the village, the town, has taken shape. The monks serve the people who, in turn, provide a variety of services for the monks, as well as vocations.

This is the one monastery in Egypt that has always been relatively prosperous, not just over the last few decades, but for centuries. Never did the population of its monks shrink to low numbers as it did in many of the other monasteries in northern Egypt. Deir el Muharraq, being *the* monastery of Upper Egypt for a long time, enjoyed all the vocations of a region of the country which was much more largely Christian. So there's a certain organic continuity in the traditions and the manner of life in this House because the customs have not been re-invented lately, as it were, but are those of a long-standing monastic practice.

The monastery has a festival every year, more or less at this time, which is called a *"mulid."* Actually, *mulids* are relatively common in a variety of contexts in Egypt. Essentially, they are religious festivals in which the lives of the founding saints are celebrated. Hundreds and even thousands of pilgrims come here every year to enjoy a carnival of food, song, prayer, and picnic-like gatherings and recreation.

At the *mulid* of el Muharraq, there are strong spiritual overtones. People here often claim to see visions, to have dreams, to hear locutions from God or the saints, and to experience miraculous occurrences in their lives. It is a place of blessings to which the pilgrims come, finding that God is somehow more urgent, more strongly present to them in the company of all of these faithful people. I'm sure that there are Moslems who likewise come because, in a certain sense, the grace of the Divine Presence, communicated by the enthusiastic and joyful assembly they perceive, transcends sectarian lines. Those who have open hearts and expanded horizons are able to obtain the blessings which may be here for them.

The monks are very busy preparing all the accommodations they must provide for the pilgrims, so I don't think that I can stay here very long, both in terms of space and in terms of services. The monks have their hands full and I don't intend to impose on them. I should have visited this monastery earlier in the year. Besides that, the heat is now really becoming oppressive. The temperature every day is well over 100 degrees or so in the shade, and it becomes difficult to travel very far or to do very much. The entire world has virtually no shade here; everything is in the sun where the temperature is even higher.

There is a cave near the monastery. There are always caves nearby, it seems. In this one, the Holy Family is said to have rested at the southernmost point in its journey when Jesus and Mary and Joseph traveled in Egypt. So it is a cave which is much visited by the pilgrims, a place of supernatural visitation where the gifts, the blessings, and the grace of God are felt by the believers of this region.

My own movement in and out of the cave was completely overwhelmed by the crush of the crowd. It was in no way a particularly spiritual event for me because, wearing a Benedictine habit, hooded and bearded, looking much like one of their own monks, I couldn't really have anything like a quiet thought or prayer of my own, but was constantly answering the pilgrims' questions and handling their issues.

Actually, the *mulid* has already been over for about a week. It lasts from the 18th to the 28th of June, but the number of people who linger for some substantial time thereafter, or who come late, is fairly great. I'm glad that I didn't come any earlier than this because, had I been here for the feast itself, or the ten days of festivities, I might have been affected by the various illnesses, especially cholera, which, I'm told, regularly breaks out among the great crowds who come for the gathering.

Over the cave where the Holy Family is said to have stayed, they have built a church, the Church of al-Adhra, the Church of the Virgin, which many Christians think is the oldest Coptic church in Egypt. The town nearest the monastery is called el Qusiya.

## A Rustic Monastery in a Modern Era

### JULY 8, WEDNESDAY

I arrived at the Monastery of St. Samuel, Deir Anba Samwel. We are not too far from the depression called "the Fayum," or "the Fayum oases." This is really one of the most remote desert monasteries, not only in Egypt, but perhaps in all the world, and surely the most rustic that I shall visit here. There are fewer vocations in this monastery than in any of the others because the conditions here are so much more rigorous. The monks here resemble the traditional monks of an earlier epoch in Egyptian history. Here are the uneducated or the less-educated Coptic monks. It is not a monastery filled with graduates who have academic degrees, but one whose monks reflect the complexion of the Coptic population living in this area of the world. These are people who spent their childhood working on farms or in craft shops in the villages throughout the upper region of the Nile. They are more rough-hewn and, in a certain sense, more peasant-like. But, at the same time, they're also very cheerful and hospitable to me. I have to share a room with several other guests in a barrack-like arrangement, but the monks themselves live in barrack-like quarters, so it is not such a terrible imposition.

The abbot had a conference with me when I arrived. He told me that he tries to discourage vocations from entering this monastery. He said that he tells the candidates to go home again, or to give up this idea, or to consider some other place. He asks if they have really been seeking God's will, or if they have been aggrandizing themselves, thinking themselves to be able or worthy to commit to this kind of environment.

I said to the abbot, "But, Abuna, isn't it your place to encourage vocations?" He answered that the life here is so difficult that if he is capable of discouraging the candidates merely by verbally challenging them, then surely life itself will discourage them much more forcefully by the day-by-day expenditure of the energy required to live here. Since he does not want them to be humiliated, to be dissuaded after having made a great investment, he thinks it is more prudent to try to discourage them before they enter. If they can overcome the assault of his words, he said, they might be more able to deal with the reversals and the difficulties that daily life itself will bring them.

I remember in the Rule of St. Benedict how the master said that monks should not be given easy entrance to the monastery. There should even be humiliations associated with gaining access to the House. So, in a certain sense, the abbot here is doing little other than what my own Rule originally enjoined. I keep remembering the slap I received at Confirmation to prepare me for adversities. This is an unpopular aspect of spiritual formation!

## JULY 12, SUNDAY

It is awful, this place. The water is more salty than in any of the other monasteries; it's so saline it's almost undrinkable. In the water are swimming various kinds of nearly microscopic fauna, so it's best that I not look too closely at what it is I'm drinking.

The weather has become even worse; now the temperature is over 120 degrees in the shade. The heat is unbearable during the day. During the short summer nights, the buildings become convection ovens because of all the sun's heat they have absorbed through the long days. The Christians, the monks, the Copts, the Moslems: everyone is suffering and is visibly weakened by the excessive heat. Many can hardly move from their beds and are unable to adjust to the temperature.

Over and above all that, there are mosquitoes here of a special kind that I have never encountered elsewhere. They are utterly silent. No telltale buzzing in one's ears before they bite. In the mornings I wake up with dozens of mosquito bites in various places which are accessible to them. I don't think I can endure much more of this place, above all the heat. But then, there is no place else to go. One would have to travel all the way to Alexandria to endure somewhat less heat along the Mediterranean coast. Even Cairo is frying in the worst heat wave of many years.

## *Of Feverish Delirium and Blessed Relief*

### JULY 15–17, WEDNESDAY–FRIDAY (POST-DATED)

By now, every thermometer I have has burst at temperatures over 130 degrees. So I am most incovenienced and discomforted in this monastery which does not have electricity, nor central air, nor, it seems, even air itself! Of course there are no fans. I became delirious, fading in and out of consciousness as we took turns going to the vat of well water to pour cup after cup of it over our heads.

The abbot of the monastery was concerned that I might die in his House, causing all the problems associated with having to remove the body of a foreigner. He didn't want to be responsible for my death, so he suggested that I make a journey outside the walls of the monastery up to the mountain where the founder had lived in a cave nine hundred years ago. This is the cave in which St. Samuel prayed, and God blessed his holiness with the foundation of a monastery under his tutelage. The mountain was several miles distant from the monastery. The abbot arranged for an elderly monk—really, quite old and gaunt, more gristle and bone than muscle and flesh—to lead me to the cave of the founder.

We left the monastery in late afternoon when the sun was setting behind the crest of a large dune, creating a little ribbon of shade across the desert floor on which we could walk. The temperature of the sand was immeasurably hot. We had to walk barefoot to the cave because we were walking on holy ground. I was disturbed to discover that my footprints were red with the blood of my feet as we walked! The old monk was walking relatively fast, sometimes beside me, sometimes in front of me, often behind me. Under my breath I was muttering and murmuring, grumbling and complaining "against God and against Moses" that I had been led out to suffer in this terrible place.

I could hear the elderly monk murmuring too. At first I paid no attention because I grimly believed that I was simply being led out into the desert to die outside the monastery. At one point the monk even threw a rock at me—at least, it *seemed* he was throwing it at me, although it went over my head. When I asked the monk why he had done this, he walked ahead and picked up the rock. Under it there was a crushed scorpion which, it occurred to me, had been poised to sting.

The monk was well aware of me, and I became progressively more and more aware of him. As I began to listen to what he was murmuring, I discovered that it was melodic. He was actually singing! He was singing a spontaneous quarter-tone song in Arabic, as a child sings, right off the top of his head! He was offering to God a song of praise! In his prayer, he was singing something like this:

"O God, I thank you and I praise you for this beautiful day
in which you smile upon us with the strength of the sun
and the warmth of your heart, a furnace of love. I thank

you for our founder who came to this barren wasteland to cultivate a garden of gratitude and praise in this house of prayer, this holy place of refreshment in the wilderness."

In this deadly 130-degree heat wave, the old monk was actually singing! He was singing a song filled with praise and thanksgiving for the wonder and the beauty of the day I was accursing! He was able to see an Eden in the midst of this wretched desert!

When we came to the base of the mountain, he ascended it effortlessly, almost as if he floated up step by step. However, with every step I took, my feet sank. For every three steps I took, I fell two steps back.

The monk reached the top of the mountain. He was an elderly man, over eighty, I would guess. And I, in my relative youth, had gotten nowhere. Finally—and then only for reasons of pride—did I scale the hill, not willing to endure the idea that this old monk was able to climb a mountain that I could not.

When I got to the top, he led me to the mouth of the cave of the founder. I didn't see it at first, as the opening was just a little crevice that we couldn't walk through. We had to slide into the cave on our knees and our bellies, some twenty, thirty, or forty feet into the earth. All along the passage I could hear the monk singing ahead of me. When we reached the interior, the crawl space opened up into a chamber. The old monk lit a small candle and then began to sing his Church's songs of thanksgiving and gratitude that we had reached the holy place, the cave of the founder.

After he had sung for what seemed like an hour or so, he asked me to sing. I was hoarse; I was dry. Our water had long ago run out as I had drunk it all in the first half hour of our walk! We were now miles away from the monastery and, so far as I knew, without water, bound to become dehydrated in a cave in the middle of the earth. The old monk said, "Won't you sing me a song of praise and thanksgiving to God? Won't you sing a hymn to the Virgin Mary from your Church so that we can offer up our praise and gratitude together?" I thought to myself, "It is better not to commit murder in this cave before my own death here." So I sang the *Salve Regina* and several other Marian hymns in which he really delighted. He asked me to sing them over and over again.

After a while he disappeared farther into the cave, and then emerged with a great pitcher of water which he poured all over me and gave me to drink. It was cool, clear, sweet water, not like the water of the monastery which was saline and stagnant, pumped out of the desert floor. Apparently, the founder of the monastery, a thousand years before, had constructed a system of fine grooves in the mountain. Once or twice during the year when it rained, every drop of water that fell on the hills would collect in a cistern in the depths of the mountain, and would be stored there.

So then I realized that the abbot had sent me to this cave, not so that I would die, but so that I would live. He had provided for me the best water there was to drink for hundreds of miles around. I also realized that the temperature in the cave was 50 degrees cooler than the air outside—a refreshing 80 degrees. It was even cooler yet as I climbed down deeper into the mountain. Before long, the old monk returned alone to the monastery and left me in the cave to recover alone.

So I lived about three days in the cave of the founder in prayer and thanksgiving until the dangerous heat wave passed. Then I walked down the mountain, back to the monastery. Tarek, Ihab, and Nasser had somehow survived the heat wave, and were relieved to see me well. We left St. Samuel Monastery in peace.

## Life Spans and Pilgrimages, Communal and Personal

JULY 19, SUNDAY

The last several days have been spent in a blur of touring abandoned monasteries in the desert of Egypt, all the way to Aswan, so I have written a variety of archaeological notes on the subject. It moves me to see fallen monasteries, broken ruins. Every monastery must surely have a certain sense of divine impulse, a sense that God himself has established it. There must be in its origins a sense of destiny, a sense that God himself has desired it. Yet of all the monasteries I have seen on the continent of Europe or in the United States, where the population of Christians is large, there have been far more *ruins* of monasteries than inhabited buildings. The failures of monasteries seem to outnumber the successes. It strikes me that even with all the bravado, all the confidence, all the assurance of the Divine Presence and visitation, human projects are often fraught with failure. We cannot guarantee the Providence of God merely by our assertions of zeal.

JULY 23, THURSDAY

I returned to Cairo directly by train. I'm preparing to make one last visit to St. Bishoi Monastery before I return to the States. I'm fairly exhausted. I think that I have somehow paced myself physically for this year, and now that my sojourn is drawing to a close, my reserves are running low. Or is it that I am merely in the psychological dynamic of anticipating a return to the States?

### *Farewell to Isaac*

JULY 25, SATURDAY

I met with Abuna Elia again today. How sweet our opportunities to discuss the Scriptures! He was crying because he had missed our meetings these past few months. I reminded him that he has all these brothers in the monastery with whom he can discuss Scripture. But, with great kindness and sincerity, he seemed to tell me that with no one else can he discuss the Scriptures as he can with me. Perhaps owing to the peculiarities of the way I was trained, or perhaps owing to the background I have in my own personal reading in Patristics, or to my family's religious background, he finds in me a sympathetic reception to his ideas and good rejoinders for his words. We really did have fruitful dialogues about the Scriptures.

He told me that I am leaving Egypt just as Isaac was given to make his departure from Abraham after they had climbed the Mount of Moriah together. Abraham was summoned to sacrifice Isaac and that, in itself, was an unimaginable horror to him. But also impossible for him to endure was the idea that, afterward, there would be no more Isaac. He grieved that the one for whom he had lived and prayed for all those decades, he would lose after the sacrifice on the Mount of Moriah.

So I was leaving, Abuna Elia said, but in God's good Providence, I would make him fruitful as Isaac made Abraham fruitful. Abuna Elia imagines that because he has discussed the Scriptures with me at length, for weeks and even months, I now contain within myself something of the core of his spirituality and the kernel of his religious life. He believes that I will make it all come to life by my own mission and ministry in the world. "You will make me fruitful," he said two or three times, "just as Isaac made Abra-

ham fruitful at last." And how can one preach unless he is sent? A
very touching farewell he gave me!

## JULY 29, WEDNESDAY

The crowds yesterday were great in the church, coming even in
the awful heat for the special blessings of visiting the monastic
church. I lingered after the Kodes for a while because so many pilgrims wanted my blessing—any monk would do. So there I was, held
captive by their coming in a line. This has happened to me again and
again in so many other contexts that I have become familiar with the
ritual of it. How abandoned we are, as monks, in the West!

### *"Out of Egypt I Have Called My Son"*

## JULY 30, THURSDAY

I returned to Cairo and am staying now with my friends, the
Kamal-Hanna family, as I prepare to take my leave. Everyone is
visiting: priests, Religious, people from the Patriarchate, secretaries, neighbors, even Moslems I have met. Everyone is now visiting this house. Somehow word has gotten out that I am leaving,
and I have a steady stream of well-wishers who come to embrace
me, to hold my hand, and even to cry at the thought of seeing me
go. It's extraordinary that my visitation could have had such meaning for any of them. But they are a warm people, and they regard it
as a grace when anyone comes into their lives, as I have, asking
questions and taking great interest in them. I'm an anthropologist;
that is my work. But my fieldwork has certainly become a pilgrimage. The two of them are now closely interwoven in such a way
that it will be hard for me to distinguish one from the other.

> *Long-Suffering God,*
> *You neither change, nor endure diminishment. You are*
> *always the same. Beyond all my imagining, you are the source*
> *of every virtue in your holy ones, and in you is all the beauty*
> *and truth by which your creatures are attractive and at-*
> *tracted. But in us is a virtue beyond all value, if we grasp it,*
> *a beauty beyond all desire, if we embrace it. Patience. Long-*
> *suffering and forbearing, we become like you. We await the*

*prize that Eve forfeited when she stole the fruit that one day
you would have given in its due season. How are you the
source of patience since you do not wait, and all time is but a
moment in your sight? How can you be regarded as indulgent
when you are supreme justice itself?*

*But your love must overcome your justice. Justice must be
tempered with pity, or we shall all die away from you. So
"long" did you "suffer" as your children languished in slavery. In Egypt they cried out, not even to your name, which
they had forgotten (Exodus 3:13). Yet their groaning reached
your ear. You bore them up, you carried them out of captivity.
You tended them with a mercy beyond the human heart of
Moses, and raised them as an infant to your cheeks (Numbers
11:10-14; Hosea 11:4). Beyond this, you endured the burden
of them when they forgot your word and rebelled against your
Law. "My people, what have I done to you; in what way have
I offended you?" you asked (Reproaches of Good Friday). "My
heart is overwhelmed; my pity is stirred. I will not give way
to my rage," you declared (Hosea 11:8-9).*

*So I turn to you now, and beg your pity. I am not at all
prepared to leave this House of Egypt to which you called me
like you called Joseph in his exile from his family. I am not
prepared to depart this place of my nourishment, as it was for
Jacob and his twelve sons when a famine covered the whole
world. My whole world was gripped in the famine of not
hearing your word (Amos 8:11), and you gave me relief in
this holy city in the desert, where latter-day Josephs have
stored the bounty of your Word in monastic bread ovens and
the ascetical granaries of your Gospel. The abbot of St. Bishoi
invited me to stay. Pope Shenouda offered me a home! They
understand me and see my joy among them. Abuna Elia
called me his only son, his "Isaac," and shared with me his
meditations from his many years of solitude.*

*How can I leave this place? To enter the monastery in
America was so much easier. To promise chastity and obedience was so much simpler. Nothing of that world could have
attracted me away from my vows or my priesthood. But the
temptation to stay here is too much for me, for, by yielding to
it, I would feel that I had finally come home to the truth of
my vocation and my vows.*

*I do not imagine, O God, that I am in any way one degree more worthy than anyone else because of the temptation to remain in the desert. Just the opposite. I know my sloth, my hardness of heart and dullness of prayer. If I stayed, I might have some respite from my sins and relief from my disobedience. Your saints here inspire me; the faith of your people convicts me. Their worship of you compels me to awaken to your Presence and submit to your Word. In the desert night and the mountain cave, I could unpack the riches I have stored up in the observance of your holy ones and the sharing of their praises.*

*I grieve, now, and my grief is the burden of my obedience. I vowed my will to an abbot far away, in the Church of St. Peter and not of St. Mark. But even Peter called Mark "my son" (1 Peter 5:13), and let him preach and die in Egypt! Even Rome would have starved but for the grain of Egypt which she robbed. May my Church be fed by the good grain of faith such as I have tasted here. May my brothers find food here as did the brothers of Joseph. Monasticism was born in Egypt; may it find rebirth from her Desert Fathers again.*

*I shall only manage to return to the world from which I came if I consider myself a bearer of the desert harvest. I shall remain an alien in the business of my future life. My eyes will be turning backward, even as I had once looked forward to a future horizon before I came here. Now I am aware that we are all "pilgrims on the earth," and that here we have "no lasting city, no place to rest our heads." Even the sorrow of this dislocation I will not be able to share. Who would sympathize, or even understand it? They shall only imagine that I am relieved to be back in "the first world."*

*I want only to be in your House (Psalm 84), and live among your people. Let me stay here, somehow, or, if not, then forgive me as I travel back, suffering the temptations of what I realize now is "the last world." In your own long-suffering, bear me up on my pilgrimage till, at last, I finally come home to you.*

# AFTERWORD

Fifteen years have passed since my sojourn in Egypt. Scarcely an hour and never a day has passed without my thoughts returning to that time. And while I have parlayed the experience into a doctoral dissertation as well as into the resources of thousands of retreat conferences, days of recollection, classroom illustrations, and pedagogical anecdotes, returning from Egypt has made me infinitely poorer than I was while living there among the monks in their remote monasteries. Though I have revisited my desert haunts a few times since then, each effort to do so grows heavier with the realization that there is no going back. God has set an angel with a fiery sword at the gate of Eden.

I hope that the poverty within my soul after all these years of dis-location since I left is of the spiritual kind that Jesus called "blessed!" I only know that it robs me, not only of what I unexpectedly found in that blessed corridor of time, but also of my ease of presence and sense of home in the present society to which I belong and, sadly, I am even less at home in the setting of the Western monks with whom I pray.

For all the burden of these transitions, however, I have never regretted the opportunities of those days. Only a grateful memory lies at the bottom of all the pain. What purity of prayer, what admiration for saints, what wisdom of ascetics, what adventures and triumphs, what humiliations resolving into faith, what filial discourse in grace—all of these were mine for the taking! Lord, have mercy, that I was not then expansive enough to generously receive what was so bountifully given. I expect to spend the rest of my life unpacking those treasures with thanksgiving.

May this little journal, a catharsis of gratitude for me, become for the thoughtful reader an extension of the blessings I once received from a beloved Desert Father.